Dup

SUR

© Giles Chapman 2006

First published in October 2006

British Library Cataloguing in Publication Data:
A catalogue record for this book is available
from the British Library

ISBN 1 84425 392 9

Library of Congress catalog card no. 2006928053

Published by Haynes Publishing, Sparkford,
Yeovil, Somerset BA22 7JJ, UK
Tel: +44 (0) 1963 442030
Fax: +44 (0) 1963 440001
E-mail: sales@haynes.co.uk
Website: www.haynes.co.uk

Haynes North America Inc.
861 Lawrence Drive, Newbury Park,
California 91320, USA

Designed by Lee Parsons

Printed and bound in Great Britain
by J. H. Haynes & Co. Ltd, Sparkford

While every effort is taken to ensure the accuracy of the information given in this book, no liability can be accepted by the author or publishers for any loss, damage or injury caused by misuse of, errors in, or omissions from, the information given.

PHOTOGRAPHIC CREDITS
B&T: 21, 56, 70, 86, 89, 96, 98, 99 (bottom), 108
BBC: 9, 24, 34, 36, 44, 50, 64, 82, 85, 124
Bentley Productions: 74, 75
Bill Krzastek: 79
Chris Capstick/RexFeatures: 94
Citroën UK: 97 (right)
Columbia/Everett/Rex Features: 28
Dean Rose: 35
Edward Hirst/Rex Features: 80
Everett Collection/Rex Features: 16, 30
Ford Motor Co: 33, 51, 127 (left)
Fremantle Media: 76, 77, 116, 117
Giles Chapman Library: 6, 7, 10, 11, 13, 14 (inset), 17, 18, 19, 20, 22, 23, 29, 31, 38, 41 (bottom), 43, 45, 48 (inset), 57, 84, 87, 90, 101, 102, 104, 105, 106, 110, 111, 112, 122, 123, 125, 126, 127 (right)
Haynes Archive: 71, 97 (left)
Howard Eastwood, Walker Singleton: 52, 54, 55
Hulton Getty: 39, 41 (top), 68
ITV: 49
ITV/Rex Features: 42
John Reynolds: 69
Kippa Matthews/Rex Features: 121
Kobal: 14 (main pic), 15, 47
Kudos: 60, 63
Lada: 37
Peter Brooker/Rex Features: 100
Peter Stevens Design: 26, 27
Peter Thompson/Hatched Brands: 48 (main pic), 99 (top)
Pictorial Press: 32 (left), 46, 58, 59, 66, 72, 73, 78, 91, 107, 114, 115, 118, 120
Rex Features: 12, 53, 92, 95
Vectis Auctions: 32 (right)

Cars TV

Star cars from the world of television

KJM 212K

Giles Chapman

Contents

Introduction

"'70s cop – Ford Granada"; that bald statement headed the flipchart at the brainstorming session that led, ultimately, to *Life On Mars*.

The creative team behind the hit BBC1 drama, in which a contemporary detective finds himself trapped in 1973, realised astutely that there's nothing quite like the right car to set the scene in television.

It encapsulates the show's style, defines the characters, carries one scene into the next, and naturally provides a centrepiece for much of the action.

Okay, so in the end they went for a Cortina, rather than a Granada, for the bewildered Sam Tyler and his politically-incorrect colleague Gene Hunt. But a Mk III Ford Cortina was a

Acknowledgements

It would have been impossible for me to complete this book without the generous help provided by these people: Gerry Anderson; Bentley Productions (Kerry Fosten); Brian Clemens; Matt Dutton/ITV; Howard Eastwood/Walker Singleton Asset Management Ltd; Tony Gale/Pictorial Press; David Hill/Ford; Bill Krzastek; Julian Leyton/Citroën UK; Dave Matthews; David Moore/Dinosaur TV (www.78rpm.co.uk); Peter Nelson/Cars Of The Stars Museum (www.carsofthestars.com); 'Nolene'/*Hart to Hart* webpage (http://users.hunterlink.net.au/~lmcvd/harts/harthome.htm); John Parnell; John Reynolds; Dean Rose; Mike Sanders; Peter Stevens; Vectis Auctions (Lorna Kaufman) (www.vectis.co.uk); Jaz Wiseman/The Morning After (www.itc-classics.com); Alan Zafer.

regular in classic TV shows like *The Sweeney*. Plus, it was the car many of our side-burned dads drove 30 years ago. So seeing one back on the box gives *Life On Mars* an extra burst of nostalgia.

Life On Mars certainly has on-screen motoring magic. So, inspired by this, I set out to recall a whole lot more of it – 49 more terrific TV shows, and the cars they drove straight into our living rooms.

The shows range from some of the earliest programmes, shown in the long-ago, black-and-white days of 1950s viewing, to some of the latest. There are dramas, sit-coms, sci-fi adventures, children's shows – many programmes you can recall like they were last night's telly viewing, and a few you may never have heard of until now (but which are probably still available thanks to the wonders of DVD).

What they have in common is a car star whose performance was as vivid, in its own way, as that of the cast. Only one, Basil Fawlty's unfortunate Austin 1100 Countryman, relates to just a single episode; no book on TV cars could ignore that "damn good thrashing", after all.

All the rest are programmes where the car plays an integral part throughout the whole shebang – ranging from Dave Starsky's Gran Torino and Del Trotter's Reliant Regal to McGill's down-at-heel Imp and even Captain Scarlet's 'virtual' Cheetah. And there are 25 more television car moments you might like to replay right at the back of the book, too.

All I can add is that I trust it stirs some great memories, and that you enjoy reading the often intriguing inside story of each of these 50 automotive artistes.

Giles Chapman

Opposite: Patrick 'Number Six' McGoohan proves he's a free man in *The Prisoner*.

Above, left: Simon Templar's glamorous Volvo from *The Saint*.

Adam Adamant Lives!

Austin Mini Cooper S

The BBC doesn't fritter away licence-payers' money on action-adventure TV series, not today nor in the genre's golden 1960s era. But in the middle of that groovy decade, viewers' appetites were huge for shows like *The Avengers* and *The Saint* over on ITV, so BBC drama head Sydney Newman, producer Verity Lambert and writer Tony Williamson decided to come up with something exciting. In the process, they concocted a show every bit as fantastical and fast-paced as the escapades of Steed and Templar, only even more charming.

Adam Llewellyn de Vere Adamant is a swashbuckling, Victorian adventurer in the Sexton Blake mould who, in the opening episode, initially set in 1902, is captured by his evil arch-enemy 'The Face', drugged, and

That luxury touch

Every 1960s celebrity craved a Radford conversion for his or her Mini, exemplified by Peter Sellers, and even running to installing hatchbacks. The *Adam Adamant Lives!* car was Radford's demo, hired by the BBC and returned after filming.

A gem that was almost lost for good

Doctor Who is the BBC's most famous time traveller, but *Adam Adamant Lives!* was one of the most watched programmes on BBC1 during its two series of 29 episodes, shown between June 1966 and March 1967.

Sadly, it's rarely been repeated because, despite being a witty and stylish show, it was shot in black-and-white at a time just before the widespread introduction of colour. The BBC assumed viewers wouldn't want to watch old 'mono' shows any more. Plus, almost half the episodes are missing from the archives, presumed forever lost.

It made a star of Gerald Harper, who then appeared for seven years in Yorkshire TV's country landowner saga *Hadleigh* during the 1970s. Juliet Harmer, meanwhile, the epitome of 1960s posh totty, had several leading parts in other shows.

frozen in a block of ice. A less intrepid soul would not survive, but Adamant is made of sterner stuff. When the ice melts, he comes to life again, but it's 64 years later.

He's befriended by foxy nightclub DJ Georgina Jones, who's heard about the courageous Adamant legend from her grandfather, and they set out to use his bravery to best advantage by meting out justice to deserving criminals. He is more ruthless than rakish, ready to slaughter someone immediately if necessary.

The lead part went to Gerald Harper, perfect for the handsome and dashing Adam Adamant, while Juliet Harmer was similarly ideal as his Chelsea girl companion and guide to the strange new era he now inhabits. They gad around London in a peach of a 1960s Mini.

This is a 1965 Austin Mini Cooper S given the Harold Radford luxury treatment, with a full-length Webasto sunroof, leather upholstery, electric windows, Cosmic alloys, and a new grille with extra spotlights. In other words, the works, plus 'AA 1000' number plates. Adamant acquires the car himself, and by episode two can easily handle its amazing acceleration and roadholding! Happily, this Mini still exists, owned by devoted Mini enthusiast John Parnell who spent five years overseeing a painstaking restoration to its authentic original specification.

This show's fun came from the incompatibility of Adam Adamant's Edwardian starchy outlook with the relaxed attitudes and sexual freedom of 1960s London, but once this had been fully exploited, for series two Adamant's focus shifted to battling his old nemesis 'The Face', who returns to torment him.

A DVD boxed set of *Adam Adamant Lives!* has been released, which features the episode *The League of Uncharitable Ladies* directed by a young Ridley Scott. For this package, Mr Parnell's Mini, Gerald Harper and Juliet Harmer came together for a video reunion; by all accounts, the stars are in as good nick as the car...

Opposite: Adam Adamant, Georgina Jones and the Mini Cooper S, given the groovy Harold Radford touch.

The Adventurer
Chevrolet Camaro & Corvette

You may have heard of the showbiz term 'star vehicle'. It generally means a TV show or movie created around its lead actor to capitalise on his or her star status. With the script relegated to secondary importance, they tend not to be much cop… as Mariah Carey recently discovered after her film *Glitter* wilted before critics and cinemagoers. *The Adventurer* was very much a star vehicle, but also has an unusual car story.

British impresario Sir Lew Grade had long admired the audience-pulling power of American star Gene Barry, particularly as Amos Burke in the 1960s police drama series *Burke's Law*. Grade pestered Barry and 'his people' to do a TV show for ATV-ITC until they finally relented. No doubt a huge fee, a cut of the profits, and a major say in the creative process swung it, and so Barry flew to Europe to make *The Adventurer* in 1972.

In this series of 26 half-hour shows, Barry plays the curiously similar-sounding Gene Bradley. Although it's never properly explained on-screen, Mr Bradley combines two careers, one as a successful businessman and the other as a film star of global repute, with his role as some sort of undercover agent. His assignments are co-ordinated by a Mr Parminter (played by Barry Morse) of British Intelligence. From this convoluted premise spring his adventures.

Gene Bradley (Barry was aged 52) came across as something of a past-his-prime medallion man, not entirely likeable and with a lecherous desire for leading ladies who were mostly in their 20s. There's something of the look of John de Lorean about him. This was entirely reinforced by his long-bonneted cars – either a red or yellow Chevrolet Camaro or else a silver Chevrolet Corvette.

These muscle machines looked slightly incongruous in scenes shot in Britain and France, but they were there because Chevrolet sponsored the show on US TV. Oddly, Bradley also turns up in a Maserati Ghibli Spider, while Camaros are sometimes driven by his foes – no doubt another of the show's many production shortcuts, which

A tall story

The Adventurer was an unhappy ship for cast and crew. As interviews with supporting actors on the recently-released Network DVD of the series prove, Gene Barry was anything but a pleasure to work with. The main issue seemed to be his stature: the diminutive Hollywood legend took umbrage at playing opposite taller actors who might nick the limelight from him, and used his star status to have them removed from the show. It was clearly all too much for veteran producer Monty Berman, for whom *The Adventurer* was his swansong.

included tired scripts, unconvincing sets and poor 16mm film stock.

Seen today, *The Adventurer* is pure 1970s kitsch, enlivened by cheesy fashions, no regard for political correctness, and one or two car chases, including a memorable sequence in the episode *The Bradley Way* involving three Citroën DS Safari ambulances – real 'star vehicles'.

Opposite: A red Chevy Camaro awaits Gene Bradley at Nice airport.

Above: Gene Barry.

The Apprentice

Chrysler Grand Voyager, Rolls-Royce Silver Seraph & Phantom

The scowling face of Sir Alan Sugar, and talented business people on the verge of tears seems an odd recipe for TV ratings, but *The Apprentice*, shown on BBC2, has been the docusoap hit of the decade. The format originated in the US, where it is overseen by irrepressible property tycoon Donald Trump, but its transition to British TV has been seamless, even down to Sugar's adoption of Trump's ruthlessly deflating catchphrase: "You're fired!"

Fourteen candidates, from all walks of business life, compete to become Sir Alan's apprentice, with a well-paid job at his electronics conglomerate Amstrad as the prize. Over 12 weeks, they group into competing teams to take on business tasks and maximise profit. At the climax of each show, Sir Alan – worth £800m, claims the *Sunday Times* 'Rich List' – fires the weakest candidate, who must walk away in shame. In both series aired so far, the final choice of apprentice has been a cliffhanger. It is, as they say, "the ultimate job interview."

During their time seeking to outshine each other, the candidates live together, and transport for their assignments comes from a fleet of black Chrysler Grand Voyagers. In this publicity coup for an MPV-maker, the chauffeur-driven Voyagers criss-cross a bustling London in pursuit of victory.

A global phenomenon

The Apprentice was created in the US in 2004 by producer Mark Burnett, and its format has since been sold around the world. As viewing figures for the Donald Trump-hosted original on NBC have dropped away, the 60-minute reality show has seen success globally, from Denmark to Dubai. The UK version, produced for the BBC by TalkbackThames, won a BAFTA award for Best Feature in 2006.

The winner of the first series in 2005 was Tim Campbell, a mild-mannered but capable former London Underground manager and in 2006, the winner was Michelle Dewberry, who went from supermarket checkout girl to business leader. The car industry itself has provided hopefuls – in 2006, Jo Cameron was a former MG Rover training manager, while Samuel Judah was a Ford engineer. Their previous experience, however, didn't benefit one task – competing to sell used cars from a giant forecourt.

Sir Alan's set of wheels for the first series of *The Apprentice* was a Rolls-Royce Silver Seraph, presumably his own. For the second series, he turns up to announce challenges in the latest Phantom, bearing his own 'AMS 1' number plates. Rolls-Royce refused to say if it had supplied the car to replace the obsolete Seraph from its pre-BMW period of ownership.

The A-Team
GMC G15 van, Chevrolet Corvette

If you can deliver a catchphrase that slips into everyday use, then something of you becomes immortal. Michael Douglas managed it twice in the 1987 movie *Wall Street* with "Lunch is for wimps" and "Greed is good", and George Peppard did well in *The A-Team*, with; "I love it when a plan comes together."

In this massively successful 1980s US action show, Peppard is Colonel John 'Hannibal' Smith, cigar-chomping leader of a group of ex-Vietnam commandoes on the run from the US military. His unit was imprisoned for cleaning out the Bank of Hanoi; they actually did this, but under order from their commanding officer. Trouble was, on returning from their mission, they found he'd been killed and his rationale had perished with him, so they were promptly jailed for the heist.

Hannibal's men include Lt Templeton 'Face' Peck (played by Dirk Benedict), Captain HM 'Howling Mad' Murdock (Dwight Schultz) and Sgt Bosco Albert 'BA' Baracus (Mr T). Hannibal rounds them up again to hit the road with him and become the for-hire troubleshooters, *The A-Team*. They choose to help those victims genuinely in dire straits. In the fifth and final series, *The A-Team* finally goes legit when the US government lifts their prison sentences in

Corvette for the face of *The A-Team*

There is another car used in *The A-Team*, a 1984 Chevrolet Corvette. This is driven by the team's resident con-man and fixer, usually referred to as 'Face' for his handsome looks and smooth talking. The car was rented from an LA agency, and the producers would apply its distinctive red stripe each time. It first appeared in the episode *The Taxicab Wars*.

exchange for the unit's co-operation on dangerous missions.

Only contactable through aliases, the A-Team members travel everywhere together in a grey-over-black GMC (for General Motors Corporation) G15 van, with a half-ton payload. The van was distinctive, with roof spoiler and sweeping red stripe dividing its two colours along the side, plus 15in turbine-style wheels painted black with red accents. It had a four-headlamp conversion and an exterior sun visor, while the customised interior boasted bucket seats, thick carpets and a large gun locker. Substantial air shocks at the back aided handling. The extra goodies were provided by Universal Studios' props experts.

Although they got through six of these vans during the 98 episodes made between 1983 and 1987 (three different registration numbers are known to eagle-eyed fans), they were hardly the stars of the show. The undoubted focal point was the inimitable, Mohawk-topped BA Baracus. He was a great character, a total contradiction in terms. When asked, he said his initials stood for "Bad Attitude". His engineering nous got the A-Team out of trouble countless times with his impromptu escape vehicles, yet he was petrified of flying.

There were plenty of shoot-outs and hails of bullets in *The A-Team,* but virtually no deaths, and most confrontations, armed or otherwise, left all involved unscathed. In car crashes, occupants always managed to crawl from the wreckage. It all represented warfare made acceptable viewing for kids – typical of the Reagan era, many think.

Incidentally, one GMC van used in the show is in fine fettle on display at Keswick's Cars Of The Stars Museum, although another is a faded wreck on the Universal Studios backlot. More trivia: the most unlikely *A-Team* guest star was Boy George.

The Avengers
& The New Avengers

Lotus Elan, Lotus Europa, Bentley 3-litre,
AC 428, Jaguar XJ12C and others

A complete set of episodes of The Avengers and The New Avengers would contain enough interesting cars to satisfy any enthusiast. Aside from the vehicles making fleeting appearances – everything from Land Rovers and Mini Mokes to a Toyota Corolla Liftback – these whimsical action-adventure shows always made use of the finest vintage and later classic British sports and touring cars.

Not that it's possible to see every episode now. First shown on ITV in 1961, the series was initially broadcast live and then from video tapes. Not every episode was even recorded, while others were later – and short-sightedly – wiped so tapes could be reused.

Moreover, the first 26 shows differed from what The Avengers later became (see sidebar). The formula Britain came to love arrived in September 1962, when debonair man-about-town John Steed (Patrick MacNee), with his informal relationship to British Intelligence, was joined by a glamorous and intelligent partner, the leather-clad, judo-kicking and motorbike-riding Mrs Catherine Gale (Honor Blackman). Together they enjoyed two years of super-stylish counter-espionage adventures, until Blackman decided she'd had enough.

At that point, The Avengers was about to switch from video to film to boost sales to foreign TV stations. Budgets were increased

Opposite: A cat-suited Emma Peel with her Elan S3 from the colour series – the car was light blue.

Above: John Steed and the white S2 Elan.

The New Avengers

The Avengers was revived in 1976 as *The New Avengers*, with French financial backing and a new twist: John Steed was now accompanied by two capable associates, action bloke Mike Gambit (Gareth Hunt) and action girl Purdey (Joanna Lumley).

Producers Brian Clemens and Albert Fennell needed a wide range of cars for on-screen scenes and off-screen film unit duties, and a deal was struck with British Leyland as the supplier. So, both Steed and Gambit drove Jaguar XJ-Ss and Range Rovers, Gambit and Purdey drove Triumph TR7s, Steed used Rover 3500 SD1s, and Purdey frequently appeared in a yellow MGB roadster. But the most unusual car was a dark green Jaguar XJ12C, for Steed, built to resemble a roadgoing replica of Jaguar's contemporary Touring Car racer.

The tie-up should have been ideal, but Clemens soon became frustrated.

"The new Rover kept breaking down and they couldn't provide us with a lookalike replacement while it was being fixed", he recalls. "I drove all the cars at least once and they were all terrible; with the MGB, you couldn't even get it into reverse gear. There was no back-up."

Of course, we now know in retrospect that 1976 was the nadir of British Leyland's problems, when quality and morale were at rock bottom. Nor did the company have much budget to support promotional activities. Alan Zafer, a former BL PR man now renowned as the producer for 25 years of The Sony Radio Awards, was in charge of what he today refers to as "product enhancement" for cars that, in reality, had serious flaws. "It wasn't allowed to cost much, or else it had to be totally free," he recalls, "but I was operating as a one-man-Jack at British Leyland. However, we did get an enormous amount of publicity."

and Brian Clemens, already a writer of many superior episodes, was recruited as associate producer and script king.

Blackman's younger replacement was the gorgeous Diana Rigg, whose character was Mrs Emma Peel, and she tackled assignments set against a background that was increasingly fantasy-driven, a colourful Britain that Hollywood could never recreate itself. "We became terribly British", recalled Clemens in 1983. "A car is a car and not an automobile. A lift is a lift, never an elevator. It is the Britishness that fits the fantasy world so appealing to Americans."

Previously, cars hadn't featured highly for Steed's female companion, although the man himself had driven several vintage Rolls-Royces and, especially, Bentleys (a green, 1926 4.5-litre tourer registered 'YT 3942' turns up frequently), chosen so the show wouldn't date quickly. Now Emma was provided with a groovy, yet elfin, car to suit her image – a Lotus Elan. In the 1966 series, the last in black and white, which began filming in

1965, it was a white, 1964 Elan S2 registered 'HNK 999C', which appeared in nine episodes.

When *The Avengers* shifted into colour a year later, the car changed hue too. Lotus provided the latest Elan S3 in a light, powdery blue, registered 'SJH 499D'. It gained far more screen time, popping up in 19 shows, and the massive popularity of *The Avengers* ensured the Elan and Diana Rigg became inseparably linked in the viewing public's mind. After filming, the car was given to Diana Rigg, who immediately sold it. After a spell in the US, it returned to the UK and is now in the Cars Of The Stars collection in Cumbria.

Although Diana Rigg is the most famous of the *Avengers* girls, she lasted just two seasons until deciding she wanted out, and for 1968 she was replaced by the dishy but somehow less steely Linda Thorson, as Tara King. In this series of shows, Steed was meant to own a maroon AC 428 convertible, registered 'LPH 800D', in place of his usual vintage machinery; as it turned out, he drove the super-powerful car just once before it was passed on to Tara. It seems, however, this 7-litre beast was considered a little macho for the lissome Ms King, and it quickly gave way to a bright red Lotus Europa, carrying 'PPW 999F'

plates, that featured in 10 episodes. In just one show, *Have Guns, Will Haggle*, she drives a Lotus Elan +2 registered 'NPW 999F'.

In 1969, the classic era of *The Avengers* closed after 161 episodes. But that wasn't quite the end of Steed's gang (see sidebar)…

Below: The third *Avengers* girl Tara King peeps nervously from her powerful AC 428.

The Baron
Jensen C-V8

By the standards of 21st century working environments, the sets for *The Baron* at Elstree Studios in 1965 must have been pretty smelly. In America, where the British ITC-made show was screened by ABC, it was sponsored by a

What America wanted

The Baron was brought to the small screen by producer Monty Berman, who cast the unknown American lead Steve Forrest with an eye firmly on securing a deal with US network ABC to buy the show. To give the smooth lone operator Mannering a British foil, Berman initially employed Paul Ferris for the part of his antique shop manager David Marlowe, but then found ABC executives preferred the character of Mannering's PA Cordelia Winfield, played by the dark, husky and beauty-spotted Sue Lloyd. Marlowe was written out and Cordelia became the regular sidekick. She gained her own on-screen car, a feminine Daf Daffodil, although it's rarely shown.

tobacco company; so the principal character, antique dealer John Mannering, was obliged to light up frequently, and preferably not at times of life-or-death panic, but when sucking on a fag might induce an expression of high-tar bliss. No easy feat, that, when facing fists or gun barrels in his role as unofficial assistant to British Intelligence.

But Mannering's car got the truly valuable exposure. He drove a Jensen C-V8, an idiosyncratic yet stylish British GT with an American Chrysler V8 engine. It was a canny match because Mannering, portrayed with laid-back smarm by US actor Steve Forrest, was an Anglo-American construct himself, based only loosely on a character created by novelist John Creasey. His nickname of 'The Baron' alludes to his Texan cattle-ranching roots. He was supposed to have antique shops in Dallas and Paris too, but the action is centred at his London branch, for which an Elstree backlot town set used in Cliff Richard's 1963 movie *Wonderful Life* doubled. The grey Jensen carried fake 'BAR 1' number plates and aficionados noted with satisfaction that its growling exhaust note was correctly dubbed.

The car appeared in the show through the cunning of Jensen's PR consultant Tony Good. His client had no advertising budget, yet Good

and dashing itself to smithereens on rocks below. It was an expensive scene to shoot, and so was reused in other ITC series right into the early 1970s, becoming a standing joke with production staff; if anyone stepped into a white Jag – often with tampered brakes – you knew it was going to end messily...

In the episode *Diplomatic Immunity*, Mannering's Jensen is seen pulling out of a parking bay outside Heathrow Airport; likewise, this footage was recycled into other shows whenever an 'airport' establishing shot was required.

had noted the widespread interest in the Volvo P1800 used in *The Saint*.

"I tried to think 'out of the box' by making it a car to aspire to", recalled Good in 2004. "We talked to TV producers, and said we'd be happy to lend them a car. The breakthrough came when we got one into *The Baron*. It was an ugly car but we did establish a certain cachet." The car used was a company demonstrator, in reality registered 'CEA 580C'.

ITC shot 30 episodes, and the Jensen indeed proved the PR man's fantasy, as it even featured in the opening titles, partly shot on the A1 in Hertfordshire, and figured prominently in most stories. *The Baron* was the first ITC programme shot on colour film, so the exposure was even more effective, although it could only be UK-broadcast in black and white.

Opposite: John Mannering and C-V8, showing its real-life registration number.

Above, left: Mock-up cabin for studio moment.

Above right: Jaguar Mk1 in that much-used cliff plunge sequence.

Batman
Batmobile

It's well known, among car enthusiasts anyway, that the Batmobile of the iconic 1966 TV series was based on a 'concept' show car called the Lincoln Futura. Designed at Ford and built in Italy in 1955 by Ghia, the Futura cost $250,000. On 3 May that year it was the centrepiece of a reception in New York's Central Park after sensationally being driven to the event by Benson Ford, Henry Ford's grandson.

Less well-known is what happened to it between times. Repainted in red from its original pearlescent light blue, the Futura starred alongside Debbie Reynolds and Glenn Ford in the 1959 MGM movie *It Started With A Kiss*.

Despite all this acclaim, the wide, shark-like Futura, with its gigantic tailfins and sinister hooded headlights, was pretty dated by the 1960s when it was acquired by Hollywood custom-car king George Barris. He hoarded it away, feeling it might prove useful sometime.

In late summer 1965, ABC asked Barris to complete a special car for its TV incarnation of comic book superhero Batman. He was given just three weeks, and Barris realised astutely that the Futura was half-way there already.

He kept the chassis and basic profile unaltered, while artfully modifying the nose section to resemble a bat-like facemask. He

then extended the leading edges of the Futura's already huge fins to evoke bat wings, and scalloped their trailing edges for an even more immediately airborne effect. The concealed wheelarches were opened up, and the car's colour changed again to a glossy black with fluorescent cerise pinstripe highlights. The dashboard and individual plastic canopies over the two cockpits, however, were virtually unchanged.

In a launch checklist read out in the opening show by Batman's assistant Robin, the Batmobile is said to have "atomic batteries to power; turbines to speed". Of course, it had nothing of the sort, boasting a Ford V8 engine, but other gadgets supposedly incorporated include a chain-slicer mounted in the nose, smoke and nail spreaders to deter pursuers, and twin parachute brakes to aid instant U-turns. It has its own miniature helicopter in the boot called a Whirlybat. It didn't need to be believable, as the on-screen *Batman* was a fantasy, like the original DC Comics strips.

The original car was in almost all of the shows, made between 1966 and '68 and starring Adam West as Batman/Bruce Wayne and Burt Ward as Robin/Dick Grayson. There were 120 30-minute shows. It made its final official TV appearance in 1979 in a special

show entitled *Legends of the Superheroes*. In that, the car was covered in flat flocking material known as 'Bat Fuzz' but today it's in its original shiny black, complete with Batman logos on the doors, and is in the protective custody of George Barris. He built three replicas for promotional use, after taking moulds from the original, and one is in the Cars Of The Stars Museum in Cumbria.

What every Batmobile must have

The 1965 George Barris design established the style for all Batmobiles since; they must be long, dark, forbidding, powerful and possess huge, bat-like rear wings. The versions in both Tim Burton's *Batman* films were in this vein, although based on the underpinnings of a Chevrolet Caprice and Buick Riviera – wild, Art Deco-influenced machines designed by Anton Furst. However, the Batmobile featured in the 2005 movie *Batman Begins* is known as 'The Tumbler', and has been described by the film's production designer as a cross between a Hummer and a Lamborghini.

Bergerac
Triumph 1800 Roadster

A few cars have become so closely associated with TV shows by the public they're well nigh defined by them. The first was the '*Maigret* Citroën' and the '*Bergerac* Triumph' was another. Or, it would have been, if most viewers had had any idea what the car actually was. A '*Bergerac* car' has come to mean a late 1940s open British car with an elegant image. That description fits the Triumph 1800 Roadster perfectly.

Bergerac was never intended to add up to much, but became one of the most successful and downright enjoyable drama series of the 1980s. In it, a young John Nettles plays James Bergerac, a police detective sergeant with the entirely fictitious 'Bureau des Etrangers'. This is a division of the police force of Jersey in the Channel Islands, where the series was set and almost totally filmed, with a remit to monitor shady visitors to the offshore tax haven and the activities of foreign companies.

Jim Bergerac does this in his own, thoughtful way. He's a recovering alcoholic and divorcee, and he patrols the island looking for trouble alone and at his own, rather stately pace in his red Triumph – invariably squinting into the constant sunshine with the roof down. Unlike other screen detectives, Bergerac has a stream of featured girlfriends, who often get

Not bad for a stop-gap

Bergerac was created by producer Robert Banks-Stewart as a stop-gap replacement for his other, ratings-winning TV detective *Shoestring*. Portrayed by Trevor Eve, Eddie Shoestring was a scruffy sleuth (he drove a battered Ford Cortina) who solved crimes often arising from his other job, as a local radio phone-in host. Eve was brilliant in the role, and offers of other parts poured in. Concerned about being typecast, he decided to give *Shoestring* a rest in 1980 after two series had gained over 20 million viewers.

The BBC asked Banks-Stewart to come up with a temporary replacement while Eve prevaricated. He'd always fancied Jersey as a setting, and so visited the island to devise the show. In the end, *Shoestring* never returned and *Bergerac* took its place, making John Nettles a household name.

annoyed with his work obsession, while Philippa Vale (Liza Goddard) is a racy diamond snaffler whom he never quite manages to bring to book, or bed, throughout the whole shebang.

BBC1 found *Bergerac* quickly became perennially popular, and in the nine series originally aired between 1981 and 1992 there were 87 episodes. However, the end was a little undignified. Public service-minded BBC bigwigs struggled to cherish such a 'commercial' undertaking as *Bergerac* and often threatened to axe it. In the final series, executive meddling saw Jim relocated to France and established as a straightforward private investigator, but this watered down the original idea and hastened the show's demise.

Captain Scarlet
Cheetah

Can there be any better partnership to create a unique TV vehicle than Gerry Anderson and Peter Stevens? The legendary producer of numerous small-screen classics, and the first-ever graduate in car design from the Royal College of Art, designer of the 240mph McLaren F1. Even better, they collaborated on a groundbreaking new series rich in TV heritage.

Gerry Anderson was approached by ITV in 1999 about remaking some of his 1960s puppet classics. A year later, he presented a two-minute film revisiting *Captain Scarlet & The*

Mysterons, made using computer graphic imaging (CGI), which was about to go mainstream in the movie *Toy Story.* Everyone who saw it was awed by its cinematic feel, and Anderson Entertainment's new series went into production in May 2003 at Pinewood Studios.

The show returned to the theme of the 1967 original: the Spectrum defence organisation and its battle to save Earth from invasion by the Mysterons. They're invisible but can use their menacing powers to take over people and objects – including Spectrum's

A thoroughly practical supercar

Peter Stevens recalls what Gerry Anderson asked for in the Cheetah: "A high-tech supercar that can do things other supercars can't. It had to work on two levels: great kids' entertainment, but also a historic attraction to grown-ups. It's not derivative but it's not utterly futuristic either." The Cheetah is a high-speed, high-grip patrol car. Concealed wings hinge down from the doors, there's a retractable tailfin, jump jets in the front wings, and rear boost jets.

Designing the Cheetah used a similar process to that of a real car. Stevens started with conceptual sketches before producing a full set of detailed plan drawings from every angle. Then, working with, Stevens says, "Gerry's wonderfully talented team, which included former product designers", the car was created in three-dimensional form entirely on computer.

"It's sensibly packaged with a realistic engineering layout", he adds, "in case we want to build a full-size car for publicity. So everything has to articulate – you can't have the doors hitting the wings if they're opened."

Unlike other Stevens designs, no 3D prototype was ever created: the nearest is a Cheetah toy as part of the show's merchandising – and a Cheetah-shaped bubble-bath bottle!

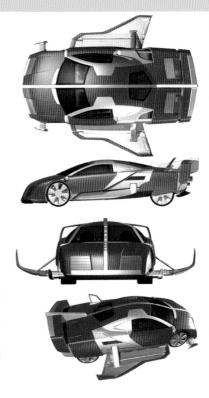

own Captain Black. The 'indestructible' Captain Scarlet is one of Spectrum's key operatives.

The old characters were painstakingly recreated digitally, but a new cast of actors was employed to inhabit them, using 'motion capture' techniques to match their real voices with expressions and body movements.

A new range of vehicles was created for the £22m production of 26 half-hour shows, and in 2004 Anderson tracked down Stevens for some advice. "I went to see Peter Stevens to find out how car designs are sculpted in clay", Anderson says. "I told him we'd be designing a car for Spectrum, and he said: 'Tell you what, I'll do it for you'." It's not a flying car – it can't travel from New York to London – but it can jump over obstacles like ravines."

Viewers are thirsting for more of this exciting TV action from Anderson and, despite being 75, he intends to keep on supplying it.

Opposite: Captain Scarlet and his Cheetah patrol car.

Above: Details of the very practical wing operation.

Charlie's Angels
Ford Mustang II & Pinto

Charles Townsend, owner of the LA-based Townsend Investigations detective agency, has a thoroughly enlightened employment policy. All his employees are women, and they're all utterly gorgeous. Well, it is 1976. And he's so keen to keep us focused on his all-action eye candy that he doesn't even appear himself. If you glimpse the unequal opportunities boss Mr Townsend, it's from behind. The instructions he gives his agents are delivered through a loudspeaker in his deserted office.

From those purveyors of 1970s lip-gloss, big hair and handguns, Aaron Spelling and Leonard Goldberg, *Charlie's Angels* came high-kicking on to our TV screens in 1976 and stayed around for five series until 1981 – 115 shows in all. In fact, it was such a popular 'franchise' (hate that word, but it says it all), that the Angels returned in 2000 and 2003 for big-screen outings in the hands of Drew Barrymore, Cameron Diaz and Lucy Liu.

But back in 1976, Charlie's original line-up was Jaclyn Smith as Kelly Garrett, Farrah Fawcett-Majors as Jill Munroe, and Kate Jackson as Sabrina Duncan – all ex-LAPD officers gone private. Ford supplied their wheels, and should have furnished the suntanned trio with some spectacular cars.

Unfortunately, however, this was the mid-1970s, at the tail end of an economic slump and the beginning of legislation's grip on car design in the US.

For this reason, Sabrina drove a Ford Pinto, the depressing little hatchback later embroiled in a controversy about bursting into flames in a rear-end shunt; Kelly was given a Mustang II, the rather grim little Pinto-based coupé that had been introduced in 1974 as the fad for 'muscle' cars evaporated; and Jill had a Mustang II Cobra, with V8 power and go-faster stripes, but hardly glamorous.

David Doyle played John Bosley, assistant to Charlie, and he drove a lumbering great Ford LTD sedan. None of these cars were particularly well considered for the characters – they were what Ford paid to have included.

The cast of *Charlie's Angels* changed constantly. Jaclyn Smith was the only Angel to star in all five seasons (and appear in the movies). First to exit was Farrah Fawcett-Majors in 1977, as it was explained to viewers that Jill had moved to Europe to (yes, really...) pursue a career as a Formula One racing driver. Her replacement, also taking over the wheel of the Cobra, was Cheryl Ladd as Kris Munroe, supposedly her sister.

The bare essentials

Turn the page if you don't want to read something rude. *Charlie's Angels* gained the notorious tag of "T&A TV" – Tits and Ass Television – because its leading ladies frequently wore next to nothing, and for no particular demand of its daft plots, either. Farrah Fawcett-Majors reckons that's why it was such a hit. She's quoted as saying; "When it got to be number one I decided it could only be because none of us wears a bra."

Then out went Kate Jackson in 1979; Sabrina went off to marry and have kids – ahhh! Her replacement was Shelley Hack's interpretation of Tiffany Welles, the daughter of a friend of Charlie. She, however, didn't fire up the TV audience so, after just a year, the character of Julie Rogers was introduced to supplant her, a New York model played by Tanya Roberts. She never made much of an impact either, though, as the show – ironically, just as popular with girls as boys – was canned in 1981.

Above: The original *Charlie's Angels* threesome of (left to right) Kelly Garrett, Jill Munroe and Sabrina Duncan.

Columbo
Peugeot 403 cabriolet

The decrepit soft-top Peugeot is one of the more bizarre choices of transport for a TV detective. but it rapidly became a trademark of Peter Falk's shuffling Los Angeles Police Department homicide investigator, Lieutenant Columbo. The glass eye, the grubby raincoat – allegedly from Falk's own wardrobe – and the scruffy 1960 Peugeot 403 were soon as

Just a few more things ...

When *Columbo* finished its run in 1978, Universal Studios' transportation department sold off the car as a surplus prop. Within a decade, however, they were desperate to get it back for the show's revival. Plans were being drawn up to give Columbo a new Peugeot, when producers finally got word of the original car's whereabouts. It was owned by Connie and Jim Delaney of Findlay, Ohio; they had bought it sight-unseen from a small ad in *Old Cars Weekly* and fortunately had maintained its original, terrible condition. The Delaneys were delighted to allow it be used in the series again.

familiar as his killer catchphrase, usually delivered with a quizzical rub of the forehead: "Just one more thing..."

Writers Richard Levinson and William Link created Columbo, and he first appeared in 1960 in a one-off NBC mystery special. A TV movie came in 1968, starring Falk, and the first series was shown in 1971. His performance was so instantly good, despite those corny quirks of a secret Christian name and a wife who's never seen, he won an Emmy for that first season. It ran for seven more years, but was revived in 1989 for a new *Columbo* series that enjoyed a further 14-year run.

Falk's Columbo appeared shambolic, but his attention to tiny clues was his métier, often allowing the culprit to give himself away. The star's mild-mannered underplaying of his role often meant he wasn't seen until half-way through the story, allowing scope for guest

stars – which have included Faye Dunaway, Robert Vaughn, Martin Sheen and even Billy Connolly – to deliver terrific performances.

The Peugeot appears in most *Columbo* shows, although the scriptwriters resisted any storyline around the car itself. It was crashed on several occasions on-screen, and it frequently broke down or fell to pieces. In the episode *Candidate For Crime* in 1973, Columbo is pulled over in a random vehicle inspection and, among other problems, he's found to have a missing windscreen wiper. "Must have lost one in the car wash", he says.

Columbo, a New Yorker of Italian origin, elects to use the Peugeot, his own car, rather than an LAPD-issued machine, and drives everywhere in it. Why he has this vehicle is never made clear (producers probably chose it to avoid upsetting potential advertisers, as only tiny numbers of Peugeots had been sold in the US), but it is without doubt the best-known Peugeot in small-screen history. The French company once ran an ad campaign stating 'Lt Philip Columbo' was its most famous customer, but it had inadvertently tumbled into a trap set by Fred L Worth, editor of *The Trivia Encyclopaedia*; Philip wasn't Columbo's first name, but rather Worth's deliberate mistake to help him detect plagiarism...

Opposite: Lieutenant Columbo with the Peugeot that never fails to let him down.

Above: A Peugeot 403 cabriolet in all its original glory – only a few hundred were made.

Left: Rare image of a US-market specification 403 saloon which, despite its good quality, made zero impact with American car buyers.

Dempsey & Makepeace
Ford Escort Cabriolet, Mercedes-Benz 500SL

This mid-1980s cop show from what was then called London Weekend Television was an undeniably entertaining way to while away an hour on a Sunday night, yet its ambitions were bare-facedly obvious. The producers reasoned there was no point in chucking their money at all the glamour, stunts and London locations that would be needed unless *Dempsey & Makepeace* could be sold to American TV. For that, they reckoned they needed to employ an American star.

Enter Michael Brandon, who took on the role of Lieutenant James Dempsey. The excuse to have him haring around London at the wheel of a Mercedes-Benz SL is that he's a New York cop sent to London on an 'exchange basis' with Scotland Yard; this is for his own good, following a corruption scandal in the Big Apple. Where he gets the dosh for the expensive sports car is unclear, but he's basically a good detective, and a tough one.

Scotland Yard's elite SI10 squad decide to make use of him by putting him to work with Detective Sergeant Harriet 'Harry' Makepeace, a feisty, blonde minor aristocrat (they'd like that in Wyoming), a former archery champion and Cambridge graduate. Their superior is loudmouth Scouser Gordon Spikings (Ray Smith), and Tony Osoba plays Detective Sergeant Charles Jarvis, Trouble is, the husky Noo Yoiker and the upper class English girl clash on just about everything, so there's plenty of emotional tension to match the action as each episode moves towards its climax of nailing the bastards.

London Weekend had in mind a replacement for its tremendously popular *The Professionals*; indeed, many of the crew were the same, and the new series kicked off with a 105-minute pilot film called *Armed And*

A hate-love relationship

The show worked principally because of the powerful chemistry on-screen between Brandon's impulsive Dempsey and Barber's analytical Makepeace. They were the best and worst of partners.

Behind the scenes, however, real-life romance blossomed between the two stars as the series was being filmed across London. If the show hadn't finished in 1986, the publicists would have had a field day with this intriguing sideshow.

Brandon (original name: Michael Feldman) and Barber were married on 18 November 1989, and their son, Alexander, was born in November 1992.

Extremely Dangerous. Dempsey & Makepeace did run to three series in 1985 and '86, 30 shows in all. After that, Brandon decided he'd had enough of brandishing his .357 Magnum on Tower Bridge. Interestingly, the show wasn't particularly popular in the US...

Opposite, left: James Dempsey and Harriet Makepeace.

Opposite, right: A rare toy set.

Catching those hoods

LWT producers put Dempsey into a Mercedes-Benz 500SL roadster. In series one and two, this is white, but it's swapped for a silver one in the third and final series.

Makepeace fared less well for glamour. In the opening two episodes, she drives a green Mini, but is then armed with that Essex Girl dream machine, a Ford Escort 1.6i Cabriolet – silver in series one and two, white in series three. Maybe it was unrealistic to have two police officers racing around in brand new convertibles, but the open-topped cars helped when filming the characters in driving action.

Doctor Who
Siva, Whomobile

Doctor Who came from the planet Gallifrey, as you know, but the yellow Edwardian car he drove in his third incarnation came from, er, Dorset.

And it wasn't Edwardian at all, but a contemporary kit car using the mechanical organs of a time-expired Ford E93A Popular/Anglia. However, its olde-worlde charm dovetailed with Jon Pertwee's portrayal of the sci-fi Time Lord, making a perfect fit with the TARDIS, his time-travel capsule resembling a police callbox from the early 20th century.

The car was a Siva Tourer, one of several models designed by kit-car stalwart Neville Trickett to come alive thanks to the thousands of old, MoT-failed Fords littering 1970s Britain. With basic mechanical skill, the £125 glassfibre kit could transform a 'sit-up-and-beg' Ford into a nifty little fun car that was easy to build and cheap to run, with the only extra component needed being a new radiator.

Doctor Who producers introduced the car in 1969 after realising many episodes in the first season of Jon Pertwee shows were set on Earth; TARDIS travel wasn't much needed, and another prop would help.

Nicknamed "Bessie", the finished car first appeared in the opening episode of *Doctor Who & The Silurians*, after the production team had expended a grand total of £342 building her, including many extras.

The public adored it, and so did the press. *The Sketch* cooed: "The car that gives you 100 smiles an hour." The show's directors loved it too because Pertwee could be prominently seen on-camera when driving, although the 'WHO 1' number plate could only be used when filming on private property, as it was owned by a Hampshire magistrate – the car's real registration was MTR 5. The car gained several tangible and intangible extras over the years, from an elongated bonnet (following an engine replacement to improve reliability) to a button-operated 'anti-thief device' courtesy of the special effects team.

Bessie straddled the divide into the Tom Baker era of *Doctor Who*, appearing in his first story, *Robot,* in 1974 and one or two later shows. Otherwise, Bessie has become a tourist attraction, now displayed in Blackpool. A permanent return to our screens is not impossible, although the Bessie image might prove too rickety for the David Tennant *Doctor Who* of today.

Story of the 'Whomobile'

Jon Pertwee drove another car on-screen, and it came to be known as The Whomobile despite its original name of The Alien.

This wild, be-finned, three-wheeled machine – something between a hovercraft and a flying saucer, 14ft long and 7ft wide – was commissioned by Pertwee himself in 1973 from Nottingham custom-car builder Peter Farries. It had a rear-mounted Hillman Imp engine, and took six months to build. The design was partly Pertwee's, and the glassfibre body was moulded in just two sections.

Doctor Who producer Barry Letts was amazed when Pertwee turned up in it one day in autumn 1973, and it was hastily written in to two stories, *Invasion of the Dinosaurs* and *Planet of the Spiders*. However, Pertwee left the show in 1974 and took the car with him. It could do 105mph and was registered for road use as 'WVO 2M'.

Driving School
Lada Riva

Well in the vanguard of the craze for 'reality TV' and fly-on-the-wall documentaries, this 1997 offering from BBC1 was to make a star of a pint-size, 55-year-old office cleaner from Cardiff, her bickering husband, and their elderly Lada estate.

Driving School was a 'docusoap', presented by omnipresent car bloke Quentin Willson,

which followed the trials and tribulations of
learner drivers in Bristol and South Wales.
Whoever else was in it doesn't matter now
because the one person who mesmerised
viewers – and there were 10 million of those at
the show's peak – was Maureen Rees. Her
incompetence behind the wheel was
extraordinary, while her squabbles with
hubby Dave were a stark lesson in always
receiving tuition from absolutely anybody but
a loved one.

We laughed as she bumped into kerbs; we
covered our faces as she pulled out into the
path of overtaking cars, and cringed as she
ran over Dave's foot. She'd already failed her
test four times before filming began, having
splashed out hundreds of pounds on driving
lessons, and producers had intended to pair
her with an instructor on screen... until they saw
what a funny double-act she and Dave made.
She failed again twice during the making of the
show, as well as flunking her theory test, before
clinching her licence in the final episode filmed
on 1 July 1997 – albeit in an automatic car, ie,
not her own Lada Riva, nicknamed Betsy, that
she'd been battling to control.

Subsequently, Maureen Rees passed her
manual driving test, and became a fixture in
the tabloids and daytime TV talk shows. Six

years later, she was interviewed by Richard
Simpson in *The Daily Telegraph*, when she
reported a generally good driving record.
However, she recounted: "I did have one nasty
incident soon after I passed my test. It
happened just as I was approaching one of
those painted roundabouts. A group of 20-
year-old lads saw me approaching, and they
mooned at me as I drove past." She also
admitted that she only passed her test thanks
to the inexhaustible patience of a female
instructor called Linda, who wrote 'L' and 'R' on
Maureen's hands so she knew which way to
turn the steering wheel, and taught her rhymes
like; "When you're round – when you're
straight, then you can acceler-ate."

Opposite: Maureen
Rees, the pupil from
hell, and her long-
suffering hubby Dave
seeming to enjoy a trip
in their Lada.

Above: What a beauty
– a pristine Riva estate
when new.

Dukes of Hazzard
Dodge Charger

The Dodge Charger certainly achieved stardom in the late 1960s and early '70s when it became the car to beat in American NASCAR racing. But it was nothing to the international fame that it would garner in *The Dukes of Hazzard* – a TV action-comedy that was, if anything, even more American than mom's proverbial apple pie.

The 'Dukes' of the title are cousins Bo and Luke Duke, along with another cousin, Daisy, and her father, their Uncle Jesse, who reside in the American deep south county of Hazzard; a place a little like rural Georgia. The clan have long been infamous distillers of illegal liquor, but Bo and Duke have been bailed to stop their moonshine activities; trouble is, these good ol' boys, while sticking broadly to the rules of their probation (they use bows-and-arrows rather than guns), just love to needle the law in the form of the local sheriff and his deputy, and the Dodge Charger provides their escape route from many a tight corner.

In the true spirit of American independence, they'll do anything to challenge authority, and love to assist friends and neighbours in bending the rules. But, at heart, they're decent guys, latterday Robin Hoods who will help those with a justifiable grievance.

It might have been hard for viewers outside

Hazzardous negotiations

The Dukes Of Hazzard was created by writer Gy Waldron, and grew out of his hit 1975 movie *Moonrunners*.

The hunky duo of Schneider and Wopat starred in the first four series, but then tried to negotiate with CBS for greatly increased fees because the show proved wildly popular. The ensuing rift between stars and network saw them replaced in series five (scriptwriters had it that they'd left Hazzard to go NASCAR racing proper) by two other, distantly related Duke cousins, Coy and Vance, played respectively by Byron Cherry and Christopher Mayer.

The original actors were back for series six but, by then, *The Dukes of Hazzard* had lost its high-octane momentum.

the USA to fathom the premise of this show, filmed between 1979 and 1985. But it didn't matter. The spectacular driving stunts and the ridiculous, dim-witted characters of the scheming chief lawman Jefferson Davis 'Boss' Hogg and his gluttonous sidekick Sheriff Rosco P Coltrane made it easy, enjoyable viewing for millions of teenagers (and adults) worldwide. It's a silly show, bursting with slapstick redneck humour, but undeniably watchable.

Bo Duke was played by the blonde John

The General Lee saga

The orange 1969 Dodge Charger in *The Dukes Of Hazzard* was known as 'The General Lee' after Robert Edward Lee, a Confederate general in the American Civil War. It had a Confederate flag painted on its roof and large '01' race numbers on each door. This was Bo and Luke Duke's high-powered automobile for high-speed fun and rapid getaways. Invariably, every episode involved some breathtaking driving, co-ordinated by expert stunt man Jack Gill, which would see the Charger, its doors welded shut, flying through the air. Only one show didn't feature the car.

The production team got through a huge number of Dodge Chargers in the making of the show, calculated by fans to be 309. They bought them whenever they turned up on used-car lots, or even when they saw them on the street. They received such rough treatment that only about 20 of these original screen cars survive. However, it was always supposed to be the same car that the Dukes' mechanic, Cooter Davenport, was fixing.

The musical horn, which plays the first 12 notes of Dixie, the unofficial 'anthem' of the South, was purchased by the producers from some kids playing it in a passing car in Georgia.

In real life, John Schneider has built several 'General Lee' replicas himself. He told *Intersection* magazine that he did some 60% of the on-screen driving himself, the rest tackled by 20 stunt drivers. "The truth is that once you've seen a 3500lb car hit the ground at 50mph from 20ft in the air, you really don't want to try it yourself", he said, before adding; "The thing I love most about the Charger is that it has almost as much torque as it does horsepower, and that both numbers are over 600."

The Hazzard County Sheriff's officers all gave chase in a variety of Chrysler-made 'B-body' patrol cars, which included 1976/77 Dodge Monacos and 1977/78 Plymouth Furys.

By 1981, the 'General Lee' itself had received some 35,000 fan letters – more than any human cast member!

Schneider, and Luke Duke by the darker Tom Wopat. Catherine Bach donned those unforgettable hotpants as Jeep-driving Daisy Duke, while Denver Pyle played Uncle Jesse Duke. The 'other side' was the thoroughly bent chief of Hazzard County law enforcement, Hogg, all down to the comic timing of Sorrell Booke, and his inept sheriff Coltrane, *aka* James Best.

The running battles continued for 145 hour-long shows, with the Dukes and their Charger thwarting every plan Boss Hogg could devise to rein them in. The already-basic concept was utterly threadbare by the time the show finished, but it was also an end to an enjoyable chapter of escapist all-American TV mayhem that's never quite been replaced.

Above: Doors welded shut and ready to go.

Below: They worked their way through hundreds of Dodge Chargers to create stunning airborne stunts like this.

The Equalizer
Jaguar XJ6

Here was an absolutely golden opportunity for Jaguar, in the midst of its 1980s resurgence after release from the chaos of British Leyland, to have its top-selling XJ6 on primetime TV across America.

Even better, the vigilante justice-seeker taking centre stage in each hour-long episode

Making the cat roar

When *The Equalizer* first aired in 1985, Jaguar Cars was enjoying an ascendancy in popularity in the US. The company had been privatised a year earlier, with a value of £300m and, under the leadership of Sir John Egan, the quality of its cars vastly improved. Products included the XJ6 and XJ12 saloons and the XJ-S GT, none of which were exactly in the first flush of youth – the XJ-S, the youngest of the trio, was 10 years old. However, in 1986, Jaguar launched its new 'XJ40'-coded range of luxury saloons, and three years later, Jaguar was taken over by Ford for £1.6bn.

of *The Equalizer* was British, played by scowling stage and film actor Edward Woodward. However, it was through the streets of New York that he prowled in the black Jag, a 1984-model XJ6 Series III with the registration number '5809-AUG'.

Robert McCall was the name of his character, a dour and world-wary 52-year-old individual who decides to take retirement from his job as a secret agent with a shadowy espionage agency known only as 'The Company'. Sick to death of the spying game and counter-terrorism, which he's been embroiled in for 25 years, McCall sets himself up as a private detective determined to give something back to society.

He's got plenty of money, so his method is to give his experience and services for free to deserving 'ordinary' people who want to see racists, wife-beaters, kidnappers and hoods get their appropriate comeuppance. People get hold of him by answering his newspaper small ad, which reads: 'Got a problem? Odds against you? Call The Equalizer, 212-555-4200'.

His contacts – often shady – from the old days come in handy, although The Company continues to exert pressure on him, which does nothing for McCall's sense of humour. The violence in the show, often rather

Woodward's cold-hearted alter egos

Edward Woodward, who was born in Croydon in 1930, was made famous by television and his portrayal of the downbeat spy David Callan in the series called, simply, *Callan* that was shown on ITV between 1967 and 1972 (and later in a TV movie and 90-minute TV play).

Rather like McCall, Mr Callan was a cold-blooded and friendless hatchetman although, unlike McCall, Callan was also somewhat down-at-heel. No slinky Jaguar for him; Callan got around incognito on the bus or the London Underground.

gratuitous, was not to everyone's taste, and was the major criticism levelled against it.

The Jaguar was a perfect match for the immaculate and slick McCall image, complete with black driving gloves and sharply-tailored clothes. However, the show is refreshingly free of gadgetry, allowing plenty of room for McCall to display his mental cunning through the 88 shows that were made and screened between 1985 and 1989.

Woodward, as McCall, always looked like he had a lot playing on his mind. But it was still a shock when the actor had a heart attack in 1987 while filming the show; Hollywood legend Robert Mitchum was drafted in for a couple of episodes while Woodward recuperated.

Opposite: Robert McCall, the 'equalizer' whose personal mission is to stand up for the suppressed and defenceless.

Above: A black XJ6 just like the one McCall drives.

Fawlty Towers
Austin 1100 Countryman

Yes, did you get that, by the way? It was an Austin 1100 Countryman. It was not, I repeat, not, an Austin 1300 estate. It's a mistake that's easy enough to make, as toymaker Corgi discovered to its acute embarrassment in 2003. As part of a *Fawlty Towers* collector's package of all 12 programmes from both seasons on DVD, a limited edition Corgi model of the car was presented, erroneously labelled as a 1300. "I should know", commented the show's producer John Howard Davies, "because I had the same car – an Austin 1100."

There were red faces all round at the Beeb and Corgi as the product was pulled so the error could be corrected. No prizes for guessing which version will be the real collector's item in years to come.

This book has tried to steer clear of cars that made only fleeting appearances in TV shows, but this red Austin is an exception, despite featuring in just the one *Fawlty Towers* episode, *Gourmet Night*. There are tons of great comedy moments in John Cleese's manic portraits of the goings-on at an erratically run Torquay hotel; the 'Germans' and 'hotel inspector' sagas are legion. But, time and again, Basil Fawlty's fevered attack on his car brings on the biggest laughter memories.

The 1100 returns in *Clockwise*

In 1986, and shortly before he rebounded to fame in *A Fish Called Wanda*, John Cleese starred in a film called *Clockwise*. This centred around the attempts of punctuality-mad headmaster Brian Stimpson's attempt to get to a conference.

It turns into an unlikely road movie after Stimpson flags down truanting pupil Laura Wisely (Sharon Maiden), out driving the family car without a licence, and requisitions it for his constantly-frustrated stab at getting to Norwich on time.

Apart from Cleese's hilariously indomitable performance as Stimpson, another link to *Fawlty Towers* was Laura's parents' car; a 1970 Morris 1100 Mk2 Super four-door, a close relative of that unfortunate 1100 Countryman, which is nearly destroyed in its journey through eastern England.

The show was created and written by Cleese and his then-wife and co-star Connie Booth, and also featured brilliant performances from Prunella Scales, as his wife Sybil, and Andrew Sachs as waiter Manuel. After just two series, *Fawlty Towers* ended, sealing its reputation as a comedy masterpiece.

Gourmet Night was the fifth episode in the first series screened in October 1975. Basil has decided to organise a gastronomic evening for the gentry of Torquay to raise the hotel's profile, but things go wrong when he discovers the chef is paralytic as the guests begin to arrive. In a desperate attempt to save face, Basil asks a friend to cook the single main course of duck at his restaurant. But his second attempt to collect the food is thwarted when his ancient Austin conks out, apparently because he tried to repair it himself to penny-pinch on garage bills.

His famous revenge attack on the car takes place on a rain-soaked suburban street. It purports to be somewhere in Torquay yet, in fact, was filmed in Harrow, north London.

Opposite: "Thrashing".

Above: *Clockwise*.

"Don't say I haven't warned you"

Here it is: the complete transcript of Basil Fawlty's assault on his unsuspecting Austin, courtesy of *The Complete Fawlty Towers Scripts* book.

"Come on, start, will you? Start, you vicious bastard! Come on! Oh my God! I'm warning you – if you don't start... (Screams with rage). I'll count to three. (He presses the starter, without success.) One...two...three... Right! That's it!" (He jumps out of the car and addresses it.)

"You've tried it on just once too often! Right! Well, don't say I haven't warned you! I've laid it on the line to you time and time again! Right! Well... this is it! I'm going to give you a damn good thrashing!" (He rushes off and comes back with a large branch; he beats the car without mercy.)

Hart to Hart

Rolls-Royce Corniche, Ferrari Dino 246GTS, Mercedes-Benz SL

Hart to Hart – the all-American dream, improbably twisted by its creator Sidney Sheldon for dramatic and suspense effect. You could tell the show was the perfectly glittering creation of its producers, those masters of the hour-long crime drama Aaron Spelling and Leonard Goldberg, for an aspirant US and, hence, worldwide audience. Somehow, though, the sparkling performance of Robert Wagner and Stefanie Powers, sharing the lead, still managed to lift the show from an ocean of perma-tanned saccharine.

Wagner, as Jonathan Hart, is the epitome of the self-made American, the millionaire owner of Hart Industries. This super-successful conglomerate is based at 112 North La Palmas, Los Angeles. His wife, Jennifer Hart (Powers), has that classic occupation of the idle rich: authoress. They live with cute canine Freeway and grizzled 'Man Friday' Max. Having, literally, everything, the Harts would surely have enjoyed a pool-side lifestyle of casinos and private jets but, maybe as they have no children, they instead turn to amateur detective work to fill those empty hours, and get a mighty kick out of righting wrongs.

True to the US mantra of success, now that the Harts have made it, the plebeian products of Detroit are banished. No Mustang or Cadillac darkens the drive of their splendidly flashy home at 3100 Willow Pond Road, LA; the Harts drive strictly imports. For Jonathan, it's the cushioned magnificence of a black Rolls-Royce Corniche registered '1 HART', for Jennifer the louche pleasures of a yellow Mercedes-Benz 450SL registered (oh, no!) '2 HARTS'. Jonathan Hart drove a red Ferrari Dino 246GTS in the show's two-hour pilot film, first shown on 25 August 1979 on ABC, but that failed to reappear when the series itself began a month later. Instead, Mr Hart was furnished with a silver Bentley S3 convertible.

The show was extraordinarily popular, syndicated in 60 countries and with 110 instalments shot in five series until 1984. Then, later in the '80s it was back as a long run of two-hour TV movies. The last was aired on 25 August 1996, 17 years to the day after the pilot movie first gripped TV audiences.

Opposite: Golden couple Jonathan and Jennifer Hart with Ferrari Dino.

Left: The Harts ready for an armed night out in their Rolls Corniche.

The Hart's motoring history

With a long-running show like *Hart to Hart*, regular updates of the cars were needed. The Rolls is a permanent fixture, but Jennifer's Merc SL is chopped in for a new one in 1981, as she trades up from a 450SL to the newer 380SL variant. The primrose colour remains, though. Sensing it was on to a good thing, Mercedes-Benz also supplied a 300TE estate for Max's household errands. In the *Hart to Hart* TV movies, Wagner has ditched his Corniche and is seen driving a silver Aston Martin V8 Volante, which seems entirely appropriate. The episode *Death In The Slow Lane* features an Albany replicar, supposed to be imported from the UK but simultaneously hijacked by smugglers.

Heartbeat
MG TA, various 1960s police cars

With 15 series under its belt, and now about to pass the 300-episode mark, *Heartbeat* has become an institution with ITV viewers, and a solid pillar of the schedules. So it's amazing to recall that the show was created in 1992 primarily as a showcase for the talents of actor Nick Berry.

Since then, *Heartbeat* has mutated into a quasi-soap opera about crime in rural Yorkshire. It is perennially sealed in 1969 and

A sad day, but a classic send-off

Tragedy struck the crew of *Heartbeat* in the autumn of 2002 when its chief 'car guru' died in a road accident.

The series' car contractor John Harrison, aged 63, was killed on the A19 in Skipton in his pick-up while he was towing a classic 1960s police car back from a day's filming.

At his funeral in York, tribute was paid by friends driving a procession of 15 classic vehicles in the cortege. Most, including the hearse, were of the *Heartbeat* period.

brims with beautiful scenery and period details, to which the 1960s police patrol cars and other vehicles seen on screen are integral..

Berry made his name in *EastEnders* before taking the part of PC Nick Rowan in *Heartbeat*, the bobby in the fictional village of Aidensfield. The series was initially set in 1964, and was inspired by Yorkshire novelist Nicholas Rhea's *Constable* books; Rhea has been a consultant to the show, although he's never written for it. Meanwhile, the village where it's filmed is Goathland, on the North Yorkshire moors, nine miles inland of Whitby. It's become a tourist hotspot, with coach-loads hoping to catch the film crew, set dressers and stars at work.

The show began as a saga about incoming (from London) PC Rowan's life, with wife Kate (Naimh Cusack). In early episodes, PC Rowan is seen restoring his cherished sports car, a 1930s MG TA; this reflected the real-life Berry, a classic car buff and Jaguar E-type owner. Berry was in the show for seven series until 1998, but over the years the programme has expanded to cover the activities of a group of

policemen based at the nearby town of Ashfordly, and their investigations into local goings-on. It now has 12 regular cast members, surely a record for a filmed drama, and has slowly shifted forwards by five years.

Moreover, although Berry left, three other characters have remained in the show since day one: sergeant Oscar Blaketon (Derek Fowlds) retired but went on to run the village pub; PC Alf Ventress (William Simons) continues to work at the police station in a civilian role; and PC Phil Bellamy (Mark Jordan) is still a goofy but likeable copper.

Peter Benson has played Bernie Scripps, proprietor of Aidensfield Garage, since 1995. Eagle-eyed and car-spotting viewers will notice that, whenever a vehicle's tax disc appears, the expiry date is always 31 December 1969.

If you don't want to see the 1960s in rosy retrovision, then perhaps *Heartbeat* isn't for you. The team behind shows like *The Sweeney* would certainly be scornful that the chummy *Dixon of Dock Green* has resurfaced in a rural setting, albeit with Northern humour.

Opposite, main: An appropriately-dressed Morris Minor ready for work around Ashfordly.

Opposite, inset: PC Nick Rowan.

Above left: Great scenery and great pre-1969 motors.

I'm Alan Partridge
Lexus IS200

Alan Partridge, the chatshow host from hell, was quite turned on by cars, rather like his speed-loving creator Steve Coogan. It must be said, however, that Coogan – although a keen driver – is not the fastest of celebrities. In BBC *Top Gear's* 'Star In A Reasonably Priced Car' feature, he was in 40th position when this was written. He completed the show's circuit in 1min

The plural is Lexi

In the second series episode *Brave Alan*, Alan is shooting the breeze with his only friend, Michael (played by Simon Greenall), a Geordie ex-soldier who works at the local BP petrol station in Norfolk.

Alan strikes up an excrutiating conversation with another customer, who turns out to be called Dan Moody, the proprietor of Planet Kitchens. The encounter leads to Alan presenting the Coleman's Mustard Bravery Awards, but it also results in the discovery that they both drive the same car – or, as Alan chuckles, "Lexi – the plural of Lexus."

53sec, well behind the leader Ellen MacArthur on 1min 46.7sec. Had that been Partridge, the inverse boasting would have been intolerable – "So, er, still faster than Anne Robinson and Richard Whiteley – back of the net!"

Partridge is Coogan's finest comic creation, the spoof sports reporter turned TV chatshow host, whose conceit and gaffes continually hamper his attempts to leave the C List of celebrityland. His appalling taste, politically-incorrect inner self, and precarious mental state add to a character whose progress through life is compelling viewing, and incredibly funny. Alan is everybody's nightmare, including his own.

A walking almanac on motorway service areas, the car he drives is important to Alan Partridge. In the first, 1997 series of *I'm Alan Partridge* – which charts his lowest ebb; he's living at the Linton Travel Tavern, with his marriage collapsed and his chatshow axed by the BBC – he's driving a Rover 820 Vitesse, to most people's mind, a terrible car. Alan is swayed by its faux prestige and dodgy sports credentials... and is gutted when, in the second episode, *Alan Attraction,* he's forced to drive a

small hatchback instead. He'd rather sack the staff at his Norwich-based company, Peartree Productions, than "drive a Mini Metro", he tells his much-abused personal assistant Lynn (the brilliant Felicity Montagu).

The second series of the show aired in 2002 and, five years on, Alan's career has picked up. His radio show on the fictional BBC Radio Norwich is no longer the 4–7am 'graveyard slot', he has a 33-year old Ukrainian girlfriend, and he's living in a static caravan while his dream home is being built alongside.

Moreover, he's moved up in the motoring world, having bought himself a Lexus, albeit the smallest IS200 model. In his usual, boastful way, he tells anyone who will listen that it's "the Japanese Mercedes." However, between the two shows, Alan Partridge did have something of a mental breakdown – at his lowest point, he drove to Dundee in bare feet while gorging himself on Toblerones.

You won't find Alan Partridge funny by reading about him. Only when you see it on the small screen will your sides split with embarrassed mirth, and fortunately both series are available on DVD.

Opposite: Alan Partridge sees his life dramatically improve with the building of his dream home and the arrival of his new 'Japanese Mercedes'.

Above: Cheeseman's choice, the mediocre Ford Probe.

Inspector Morse
Jaguar MKII

Inspector Morse passed away on the small screen in November 2000, his final words being: "Thank Lewis for me." Less than two years later, in February 2002, John Thaw, the actor who played the beer-drinking, opera-loving, sometimes morose detective created by Colin Dexter, followed him to the grave in real life. For the series' millions of devotees – and for Kevin Whately, who played his sidekick Sergeant Lewis – it was all terribly sad.

But at least one iconic element of the whole *Inspector Morse* phenomenon has been rejuvenated, and in spectacular style. Morse's faithful classic Jag emerged from a painstaking restoration, its components pieced back together as carefully as the clues in one of Dexter's elegant plots. What's more, the car was sold in November 2005 in an auction that saw bidding climb to just under £150,000 – making it the most valuable Jaguar MkII ever.

It's now a world away from the shabby heap that made its debut in the opening Morse episode in 1987. Registered '248 RPA' in Surrey in 1960, the Jaguar 2.4-litre MkII had been purchased from a scrapyard by the props team working on the Central TV series. Apparently, it had to be pushed into

Morse gets everyone's stamp of approval

Inspector Morse is an extraordinarily popular show. The series was voted the fourth greatest ITV programme ever in one poll, leading the Royal Mail to illustrate the Jag and Morse on one of five commemorative stamps issued in September 2005 to celebrate ITV's 50th anniversary.

In another survey, in July 2004, it beat the *Italian Job* Mini Coopers, Chitty Chitty Bang Bang, and James Bond's Aston Martin DB5 to become Britain's all-time favourite 'famous car'.

The saving of an icon

Restorer David Royle was responsible for the costly makeover of Morse's Jag.

"It was drivable when delivered to us but, in fact, was in very poor condition", he recalled. "So we systematically dismantled and stripped it, and found numerous old repairs, patches and bodges. The damaged and corroded parts of the body were replaced, and all the mechanical components reconditioned, with the engine converted to use unleaded petrol. However, the interior woodwork, upholstery and carpets have simply been cleaned and retained."

Royle's team retained unique Morse details, like that vinyl roof and even a special bracket attached to the front of the chassis, used for mounting cameras during filming.

Above: It's a bracket, but not just any old bracket – expert David Royle was careful to retain unique details like this camera mount when undertaking restoration.

place in several scenes because it was a non-runner, and up-close it was obviously a pretty ropey specimen, despite the buffed-up paintwork. Jaguar connoisseurs winced at the tacky vinyl roof covering glued on by one of its four previous owners.

The producers did get it running eventually, but precious little was spent on the car – just enough to make it look convincing

for the hours of footage shot of the Jag rolling through the streets of Oxford and local country backwaters where Morse did his laid-back sleuthing.

This car, and only this car, was used in every episode of *Inspector Morse* from 1987 until 2000. The final episode, *The Remorseful Day*, was seen by 12 million viewers in the UK.

Once the cameras stopped rolling, Central

didn't need the Jaguar any more, and it was raffled in a Woolworth's promotion in November 2001. The winner, a London lawyer, didn't want it either because he sold it in April 2002, and then it was sold again, fetching £53,200 at auction. The buyer owned a property company in Gateshead, Tyne & Wear, and when that went into receivership in 2003, the Jaguar went with it.

At that point, the car, which had covered 79,460 miles, had already spent almost a year in the 'car hospital' of restoration company David AC Royle & Co in County Durham, and receivers BDO Stoy Hayward sanctioned its completion in June 2005. Its eventual new owner, Ian Berg, pledged to keep the car in the UK and to give wistful *Inspector Morse* fans regular opportunities to see it.

Above: '248 RPA' is probably TV's most famous Jag ever.

Jason King
Bentley S-type Continentals

Jason King is a kitsch classic; a series of 26 lightweight, hour-long mysteries about a flamboyant playboy who's the creater of his own fictional detective, Mark Caine, and whose skill at criminal plotting means he's perfect for sleuthing himself. Indeed, he's obliged to help solve crimes by the British government which holds tax-evasion charges against him as a bargaining chip. Sounds unlikely? That tells only half the involved on-screen story...

The King character had first appeared in *Department S* (see sidebar), screened two years before *Jason King* was shown on ITV between September 1971 and April 1972, and had proved so popular in the hands of actor Peter Wyngarde that the spin-off was created. Wyngarde, until then a character actor specialising in splendidly sadistic villains, had imbued King with his own larger-than-life persona – to the point where, as James Chapman says in his book *Saints & Avengers: British Adventure Series of the 1960s*, he became "surely the most absurdly camp hero in the history of television detectives." His ultra-groovy clothes were an

inspiration to Mike Myers for his satirical
comedy alter ego Austin Powers.

Even the character's creator, scriptwriter
Dennis Spooner, had misgivings: "I thought the
failing of *Jason King* would be just what it turned
out to be – that in big doses, he would be too
flamboyant." King lived a life of champagne-
fuelled excess, based in Paris and travelling
throughout Europe. Chain-smoking and
constantly hung-over, he still appeared to
have plenty of energy to bed a stream of
gorgeous girls.

And wheels? Surprisingly, Jason wasn't
equipped with a Jaguar E-type or Lamborghini
Miura, but an uncharacteristically subtle car. He
had a silver-green Bentley S2 Continental, with
'notchback' two-door, four-seater body by HJ
Mulliner. It bore black-on-white number plates
reading 'BE 20838'. *Jason King* shows are
sprinkled with footage of this car driving around
Paris, but the plates weren't French and the car
was right-hand drive.

Wyngarde's Jason King had also driven a
Bentley in *Department S*, but not the same car.
It was a maroon four-door Continental S2 with
coachwork by James Young that's often
referred to as that company's 'Flying Spur'
style. It was also registered 'BE 20838', but was
'11 PPO' in real life. You can catch it in the

The unfortunate downfall

*Department S (*28 episodes were made in 1968 by ATV-ITC,
and shown on ITV in 1969) was the forerunner of *Jason
King*; an adventure show featuring an Interpol team solving
baffling cases. They were King, computer expert Annabelle
Hurst (played by Rosemary Nichols) and tough guy Stewart
Sullivan (Joel Fabiani). Their boss was Sir Curtis Seretse
(Dennis Alaba Peters), unusual then for representing a
black person in authority. The Jason King character proved
very popular with female viewers. But, pre-dating George
Michael's 'incident', the ladies' man image was shattered in
1975 when Wyngarde was convicted for committing an "act
of gross indecency" in the lavs at a Gloucester bus station.

episodes *The Double Death of Charlie
Crippen*, where King arrives at an Italian villa
and tries to wangle his way in, and in *The Last
Train To Redbridge*, where police stop the car
on the A1 to pass King a message.

Below: Jason and
Porsche 911 during
shooting at Elstree.

Knight Rider

'KITT' Pontiac Firebird Trans-Am

Few action dramas have been as much a 'car' show as *Knight Rider*. After all, one of the main characters was itself a car. Its creator, Glen A Larson, has said: "I wanted to do *The Lone Ranger* with a car... a kind of sci-fi thing with the soul of a Western."

The main protagonist here is Michael Knight. Formerly undercover cop Michael Long, his recovery from a neat-fatal gunshot to the head is assisted by FLAG, the Foundation for Law And Government, a private crime-fighting organization backed by ailing millionaire Wilton Knight and based in southern California. Not only is he equipped with a remodelled face, improbably handsome of course, but he is sent on justice-seeking missions with KITT,

standing for Knight Industries Two Thousand, the ultimate in high-tech cars. No shoot-'em-up guns for Knight; KITT uses his phenomenal electronic brain and stunt-car dynamics to outwit their opponents. It was never mentioned explicitly in the show (see sidebar), but KITT was obviously based on the third-generation Pontiac Firebird Trans-Am, introduced during the same year the show made its debut on NBC, 1982.

David Hasselhoff, then a relative unknown but later to find worldwide stardom in *Baywatch,* takes the role of Knight. In addition to the obvious villains and dishy young heroines featured in most of the 90 shows made in four series until 1986, the other regular character was Devon Miles, an uppercrust English defence and tactics guru (portrayed by the late Edward Mulhare) who acted as Knight's handler. Patricia

McPherson and Rebecca Holden plated KITT's glamorous mechanics.

The softly-spoken and often sarcastic KITT (voiced by actor Williams Daniels), essentially the computer brain inside the car, could use its artificial intelligence to drive itself and keep in contact with Knight through a 'comlink' masquerading as his watch. The car was armoured to withstand anything up to heavy artillery, could manage 200mph (upped to 300 in the final series), and could use its 'Turbo Boost' to leapfrog over danger. Or so it appeared on screen.

In fact, the stunts, coordinated by Jack Gill, used four Firebirds. One radically-lightened version was used exclusively for the jumping sequences, and was given a smooth plastic underside for when it was hoisted aloft by a crane and filmed from below.

Opposite: The red flashing bonnet scanner was a distinctive feature of KITT in Michael Scheffe's makeover of the Pontiac Firebird.

Above: David Hasselhoff, later of *Baywatch* fame.

Life On Mars
Ford Cortina MKIII

It's enough to gladden the heart of any petrolhead: when the creators of *Life On Mars*, Matthew Graham, Tony Jordan and Ashley Pharoah, traipsed off for a 'creative session' in Blackpool to come up with a new show, they kept returning to one theme.

"There is still photo evidence from their brainstorming (or should that be drinking) session", says Claire Parker, the producer. "They had a flipchart with the words ''70s cop – Ford Granada' scrawled on it."

As you can imagine, they had classic shows like *The Sweeney* in mind, but a remake would not be very mainstream, and if done with authenticity would be far too politically-incorrect. So they had the brainwave of transporting a cop from today back to the police era of the early 1970s and exploring the two, very contrasting worlds. In coming up with the idea, they found they had the surprise TV drama hit of the year on their hands, eagerly watched and glowingly reviewed when the first season began in January 2006 – stuffed with action and wit.

It's also, it must be said, as unlikely a scenario as any dreamed up by television; as implausible as *Randall & Hopkirk (Deceased)* or *Knight Rider*, and something of a return to the concept of *Adam Adamant Lives!*

1973, and all that

"I had an accident and when I woke up I was here", Sam Tyler tries to explain. "Only here is 32 years in the past. Now that either makes me a time traveller, a lunatic, or I'm lying in a hospital bed in 2005 and none of this is real."

The 1973 that Tyler had crash-landed into was the time of the three-day week, with 50mph speed limits and the evening's telly viewing ending at 10.30pm to save energy. Acts like Suzi Quatro and David Bowie ruled the music scene. Children stuffed their faces with Ringos and Curly-Wurlys, and the Chopper bike was every teenager's dream.

John Simm is Sam Tyler, a Manchester detective whose private life is becoming entwined with his work after his girlfriend is kidnapped by a wanted killer. As the pressure on him swells, he's involved in a near-fatal car crash in his SUV. The impact is sudden and violent enough to put him into a coma, yet Tyler finds himself stepping from the wreckage to discover that he has, somehow, been transported back to 1973.

Tyler is as confused as anyone would be in such a dream-like situation, but his bloke-ish police colleagues don't have much time to listen to his ramblings. There are villains to catch and they're going about it in the only way

Opposite: Wonder if that handset came from an early branch of Carphone Warehouse? Gene Hunt, talking, with Sam Tyler and the super-cool Cortina MkIII.

'He's got one – where's mine?'

The central figure of *Life on Mars* doesn't get to loon around in the Cortina, to his chagrin.

"Everyone on set wanted the Ford Cortina; it became quite a coveted item", says John Simm. "Screeching car chases, fantastic! Unfortunately, I didn't get to drive it because it was Gene's car and I didn't have one, which is unfair. Hutch from *Starsky & Hutch* had a car; it was a knackered car but he had a car all the same. Maybe a Capri or something would be nice."

Philip Glenister himself found the old car to be a bit of a handful.

"It was very difficult to handle without power steering", he says. "I was rather shocked by it. It was a rustbucket really, so when it's not your car you can throw it around a bit. It was great fun, quite a flash motor for the time, although I always wanted Tony Curtis's Ferrari Dino [from *The Persuaders!*].

"I did as much of the stunt work as I could. Peter, our stunt co-ordinator, was keen to let me do as much as possible. I was putting my foot down, slamming on the brakes and trying to hit certain marks, which meant I had to do several rehearsals to get it right.

"But I'd hate getting back into my car on the weekends, because I'd be driving with my missus and she'd say: 'You're driving awfully fast, dear, can you slow down? You can do it at work, but this is Richmond!'"

they know how – with minimal technology, plenty of brute force and buckets of coppers' gut instincts, all finished off with plenty of booze, fags, bigoted remarks and gratuitous sexism. In any contemporary drama, that would be unacceptable, but this, after all, is 1973. The absence of the aids to modern policing – computers, forensics and legal procedures – leaves Sam Tyler feeling more helpless still, as he feels revulsion at his colleagues' methods. Only WPC Annie Cartwright (Liz White) helps him get through his new/old world malaise.

And what about that Ford Granada? Well, the top model in Ford's 1970s range never made it into the finished show. Instead, DCI Gene Hunt (a rollickingly rude performance by Philip Glenister) tools around in a metallic copper Ford Cortina MkIII 2000E, a car that certainly is familiar from cop shows of the period.

Authentic as it looks, however, sharp-eyed pedants have already pointed out some anomalies. The Cortina used has a GXL badge on the front grille and, for some reason, a dashboard from a MkIV Cortina. Meanwhile, an Austin Allegro panda patrol car regularly seen in the show is an Allegro 3 version, only current from 1979 on.

There's no pleasing some people...

Below: Gene's bewildered by his colleague, Sam's just plain bewildered all round, and anorak viewers aren't sure if that's a 2000E or a GXL.

Lovejoy
Morris Minor Convertible

Expensive to shoot

The 'action car co-ordinator' on *Lovejoy* was Peter Thompson.

"Lots of the cars we used were British, like the Land Rover Discovery, Range Rover, Jaguars and Rollers," he recalls, "But I was also the first person to put a Jeep Cherokee on British TV in the show.

"The Morris Minor, however, we actually bought for the production – it was a prop. There was just the one car, and I acquired it afterwards. The show was filmed all over Suffolk, with a crew of 60 who all had to be accommodated, catered and transported. It cost a lot to make, as you can imagine, which is why this type of show doesn't really exist any more. Filming on location is very expensive... and 'tight' scenes, which fill the screen with the actors' faces, don't need much background and are therefore much cheaper to film."

In the original *Lovejoy*, Ian McShane played the eponymous antique dealer with a rogue-ish edge that was entirely appropriate. The character was based on the one in the novels of Jonathan Gash, and he really was a shady piece of work. Like Gash's character, McShane's Lovejoy has done time for his dodgy activities, although the TV iteration was still something of a latterday Robin Hood, and also a hopeless romantic.

The show was first aired in 1986, and Lovejoy initially appeared on the screen in that antique dealer's stalwart, the Volvo 244 estate. It was a particularly battered example, always letting him down. In the second series, and after release from prison, he's given a battered, Trafalgar blue Morris Minor convertible by Lady Jane Felsham (played by Phyllis Logan), a local aristocrat who has a soft spot for the cheeky Lovejoy. The car was exhumed from its longtime resting place in a garage on the Felsham Hall estate. His nickname for it is "Miriam". In this car he roams the Suffolk countryside where the show is set, helping out those he thinks need it and hoodwinking those others – especially the most insidious antique dealer rip-off merchants – whom the impish Lovejoy (yep, it's that fiction-writer's fallback cliché again – we never get to know his first name) thinks deserve it.

The travails of a 'divvy'

It was Ian McShane himself who spotted the televisual potential of Jonathan Gash's Lovejoy character and brought him to the screen. A TV and film actor of repute, McShane was himself perfect for the leading role, and the first 10-episode series was well liked in 1986. McShane's character was a 'divvy', short for diviner, a dealer who can spot the one artefact of decent value in an attic full of trash. "It's the genuine article, Tinker," he would say to his assistant, "I can feel it."

However, for contractual reasons, a second series did not follow until almost five years later in 1991. Although the show was a little less spicy now, the producers cranked out 61 more shows and feature-length specials in five series in the space of just three years. The main differences in this second tranche of outings – apart from the introduction of the Morris Minor – was Eric's departure to run a pub, and the arrival of auction house graduate Charlotte Cavendish (Caroline Langrishe) to replace Lady Jane Felsham as Lovejoy's object of lustful desire.

The excellence of *Lovejoy* was a cocktail of McShane's acting – which included 'breaking the fourth wall', film industry speak for addressing the viewer directly by talking straight to camera – Ian Le Frenais's scripting polish and the stunning locations picked from all over Suffolk.

Not to be underestimated, however, is the contribution from Lovejoy's two reprobate sidekicks, the intelligent but alcoholic Tinker Dill (seasoned character actor Dudley Sutton), and the thick if eager Eric Catchpole (Chris Jury).

Opposite: Appealing rogue Lovejoy is back on the road after a spell in stir, now behind the wheel of Miriam.

Magnum PI
Ferrari 308 GTS

It really did exist (almost)
Who wouldn't like to live like Magnum;
free use of the Hawaiian beach-front
estate and Ferrari of mysterious writer
Robin Masters (we never get to see
him, but his voice is provided by none
other than Orson Welles), a fridge
constantly stocked with cool beer,
and more attractive women than you
can shake a snorkel at.

Indeed, the apparently 'Robin's
Nest' location at Road 72 off
Kalania'ole Highway, Wairmanalo
Beach, Hawaii, really does exist,
complete with the main mansion,
Magnum's guest house, tennis court
and tidal pool. Only the interiors were
shot inside Universal's Hollywood
studios, but the show also recycled
sets and props used in the long-
running *Hawaii Five-O*.

With all this TV screen eye candy
in place, a huge number of episodes
were shot, totalling 162 by the time
the show ended in 1988.

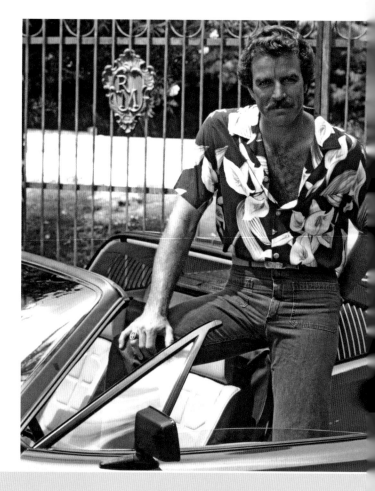

Tom Selleck is Thomas Sullivan Magnum III, Private Investigator, a man who has adjusted reasonably happily to life after his time fighting with the US Navy in Vietnam. He is a resident of a private beach house where he's employed to look after security. The place is run by sniffy Englishman Jonathan Quayle Higgins (Texas-born actor John Hillerman), constantly referred to as "Higgy Baby" by Magnum. Selleck's character is frequently seen sporting a Hawaiian shirt and Detroit Tigers baseball cap, although he is, perhaps, even more memorable as TV's most prolific Ferrari driver.

Throughout the entire run of *Magnum PI,* from 1980 until 1988, Magnum is seen at the wheel of a Ferrari Dino 308 GTS. In fact, this could be one of three cars, because filming began with a 1979 308 GTS, transferring to a 1981 308 GTSi and then a 1984 328 GTS QV. Known serial numbers are '29109' for the first car, '34567' for the second and '57685' for the final one. As they all looked near-identical, though, this didn't make much difference to the public – apart from the car in the pilot episode, registered '56E-478', they all carried the number plate 'ROBIN-1'. In the US and elsewhere, the car became so inextricably linked to Selleck's wisecracking, medallion-man character that it was universally known as "the *Magnum PI* car".

It also introduced the idea of a Ferrari as a dream ride to a whole new generation.

Selleck is an extremely tall chap, and would have had difficulty squeezing himself in to the standard offering from Maranello. So the Ferraris had modified cockpits, with the driver's seat bolted into position as far away from the steering wheel as possible, and the padding taken out of the cushions, so Selleck could be filmed sitting in the car without his head poking out of the Targa top. He also told interviewer David Letterman in 1997 that the first car had a viciously stiff clutch, resulting in one or two starts that had the production crew fleeing for their lives!

It's said that up to five examples of each of the Ferraris were used for various aspects of filming, ranging from close-ups to high-speed chases. It's also claimed that a bedraggled looking 'Ferrari' that sits on the backlot at Universal Studios is no such thing, but in fact is a kit-built replica used for particularly rough stunts.

Certainly the cars pop up for sale from time to time, and one of them – the GTSi – has found a resting place at the Cars Of The Stars Museum in Keswick, Cumbria. Another was bought by actor Larry Manetti, who played one of Magnum's ex-Vietnam War buddies, Orville 'Rick' Wright.

Maigret
Citroën 15-Six 'Traction Avant'

"The *Maigret* car": have you ever heard that said, or read it in a magazine or newspaper, and wondered what on earth was meant?

The phrase has become British shorthand for any example of the 1934-57 Citroën 'Traction Avant' (meaning 'Front-Drive') series, and especially any model painted black. This all comes down to the fact that just such a black Citroën was featured in the BBC TV series *Maigret*, screened between 1960 and

1963, and it was enjoyed by millions of viewers every week.

'Commissaire' Jules Maigret was the literary creation of Belgian writer Georges Simenon. He was an earthy Parisian detective, a compassionate man, but also an extremely dogged and intuitive one. He would work his way quietly through a case until the suspect couldn't fail to give themselves away. Simenon sold the rights to his work all over the world, and there have been Austrian, Irish and even Japanese actors filmed in the role of his sleuthing hero. However, it was the BBC that made the definitive TV version, by critical agreement as well as in the mind of the author. French TV bosses were so impressed, that a dubbed version was sold back to the domestic network. Apart from the extremely well-crafted feel of the show, its success was down to the near-perfect casting of British actor Rupert Davies as the man himself. From the moment Maigret struck a match on a wall to light his pipe in the opening credits, accompanied by Ron Grainer's splendid accordian theme music, you knew you were in for compelling entertainment. There were 52 stories in all, varying between 45 and 55 minutes long.

The Citroën that Davies drove was built in 1954, a six-cylinder, 15-Six, model which is also known in Citroën circles as a 'Big Six'. It was left-hand drive, a Parisian-built car as opposed to one of the many assembled in the UK at Citroën's Slough plant, and it featured DS-style hydropneumatic suspension at the rear.

Interestingly, Davies acquired the car after relinquishing the Maigret role and, although he sadly died of cancer, aged 60, in 1976, the car is known to have stayed in the possession of his family to this very day.

The show, like other elderly TV gems such as *The Forsyte Saga,* has been rarely seen because it was shot in black and white. However, ITV offered a colour remake in 1992 with Michael Gambon as the Citroën-driving detective. While a perfectly acceptable period drama, it failed to fire the viewing public's imagination as the sultry original had.

Opposite: Rupert Davies in the car he eventually owned.

Above, top: Gambon's lukewarm remake.

Above: Maigret, pipe-smoker extraordinaire.

Man In A Suitcase
Hillman Imp

Actor Richard Bradford, in his role as McGill in this superb 1960s detective series, genuinely raised the standard for gritty, brooding performances in the genre. He did not, it must be said, do much for the image of the Hillman Imp.

Man In A Suitcase follows the itinerant, American McGill (we never discover his first name, although his few friends call him "Mac") as he ekes out a living as a private investigator, a gun for rent if needs be. His assignments are often unpleasant and the people who hire him sometimes treat him with disdain.

For McGill has a dark secret: he was dishonourably discharged from the CIA. He seethes with anger at the injustice of it all. Forced to work in Europe, and based in London, his resourcefulness and integrity nevertheless make him eminently employable.

He doesn't need much to survive, avoiding commitment and living in cheap hotels and rented flats. Everything he has can fit into his battered suitcase, and the Hillman Imp is his downbeat choice of wheels. In fact, he drives several examples of the little rear-engined car in green and red, but is also seen using a Trumph Herald estate and a Ford Zephyr MkIII.

The Imps, and the other cars, are just the tools of the job for McGill. In the episode *The Sitting Pigeon*, McGill is assigned the task of looking after convicted gangster Rufus Blake (a terrifically nasty performance from George Sewell) for a day in a police-instigated scheme to acquire incriminating evidence. The dialogue was typically abrupt:

"Is this the best you could do, this heap of junk?" sneers Blake.

"Well, it won't attract too much attention", retorts McGill.

"I thought you Yanks liked flashy cars. This one's for peasants."

"Well, that's us."

Blink and you'd miss the switch

There's a fascinating car-related example of how corners used to be cut on TV long before the advent of the VHS and DVD player could detect them.

In the *Man In A Suitcase* episode *Somebody Loses, Somebody... Wins?*, McGill is forced to blast his escape through the border control between East and West Germany in a Russian Moskvich car. In the hail of bullets that follows him as he smashes through the East German checkpoint, the car catches fire.

However, the Moskvich was a rare and useful film and TV prop at Pinewood Studios – far too precious to destroy. The car goes up in flames, but it is switched mid-way through the scene for the burning carcass of a Ford Prefect that has been given an identical grey-and-green paint job.

The concept, the scripts, the direction, even the rousing theme tune by Ron Grainer (which got a renewed lease of TV life as the theme for Chris Evans' *TFI Friday*) – everything about this 1967 show was cracking. But the best part was Bradford's tough, brooding and utterly compelling portrayal of McGill.

Handsome, yet vulnerable, and with a head of prematurely grey hair, Bradford was a stickler for the 'method acting' perfected by his friend Marlon Brando. The British production crew and the often-'stagey' British supporting actors were bemused at how much effort Bradford lavished on his craft to make McGill's actions appear realistic.

Too bad, then, that an indifferent response from viewers in the US meant only a single series of 30 episodes was made.

Opposite: He's cool, he's calculating and he's downbeat – McGill turns up for another job in his Hillman Imp for "peasants."

Above left: Original Imp is an admired classic to some, but glamorous it is not.

Miami Vice
Ferrari 'Daytona' & Testarossa

Detective James Crockett's dishevelled appearance, unshaven and with a T-shirt on under his pastel-coloured, sleeves-rolled-up jacket, was a seminal 1980s style statement. And *Miami Vice* was one of the best and most exciting cop shows of that exuberant decade. It drew its pace from a Universal Studios edict that they wanted to produce an 'MTV cops' type of show.

The cars that appear in it, however, proved highly controversial.

Don Johnson's Crockett enjoys an apparently high-octane lifestyle thanks to the Miami-Dade County Vice Department. As 'Sonny Burnett', he lives on a yacht, uses a speedboat and drives a Ferrari around the sun-drenched Florida resort. However, all these 'toys' are part of his undercover image as one of the drug-runners he's tasked with catching; moreover, the boats and cars have not been paid for by Miami's reluctant taxpayers, but are all trophy assets that the police have confiscated from felons.

His Ferrari is a black 365 GTS/4 Daytona Spider, sporting the Florida licence plate 'ZAQ 178'; in the show, it could have been one of the prized originals or, possibly, one of the many US conversions. It certainly put in some

NEW MUSIC FROM THE TELEVISION SERIES, "MIAMI VICE"
STARRING DON JOHNSON AND PHILIP MICHAEL THOMAS

MIAMI VICE II

FEATURING
JACKSON BROWNE
PHIL COLLINS
THE DAMNED
JAN HAMMER
STEVE JONES
GLADYS KNIGHT
and THE PIPS
PATTI LA BELLE
and BILL CHAMPLIN
ROXY MUSIC
ANDY TAYLOR

Left: Albums of *Miami Vice* music stormed the charts and broke sales records – note the new Ferrari Testarossa.

spirited performances chasing villains through the Miami streets.

In fact, it wasn't a Ferrari at all. It was a McBurnie replica, built using a 1980 Chevrolet Corvette as a base, with a completely fake body and interior that incorporated a few genuine Ferrari parts. According to *Motor Trend* magazine, it was one of two that had once been seized by the US government in a complex legal deal.

Miami Vice became a huge global hit, but the show's popularity proved uncomfortable for Ferrari itself, as viewers believed that the car they saw flashing across their TV screens was a genuine Daytona Spider – one of the world's most desirable classic cars. A solution was found by offering the producers two brand new, 180mph Ferrari Testarossas for the third season in autumn 1986. In the opening show, Crockett's beloved Daytona is blown up by a Stinger missile launched from a black Testarossa, and in the following show Crockett's superior Lieutenant Castillo hands his still distraught operative the keys to a brand new Testarossa in white, with the licence plate 'ATF 00M'. A third car, a Testarossa lookalike based on an old De Tomaso Pantera, was constructed for stunt work, and by agreement with Ferrari, this vehicle was destroyed when

the show finished in 1989, while the white Testarossa is on display at the Swap Shop Flea Market in Sunrise, California.

Having the Testarossa in the series produced such great exposure for Ferrari that the Italian company gave a silver example to Don Johnson as a gift in 1989.

Miami Vice nuggets that are cool to know

- A soundtrack LP from the show topped the album chart for 11 weeks in 1985 – the best-selling soundtrack record ever, beating Henry Mancini's 1959 *Peter Gunn* by a week.
- Crockett lives on a 42ft yacht, an Endeavour 42 called *The St Vitus Dance*, and uses Criss Craft and Wellcraft 'cigarette' speedboats to commute to and from it.
- A movie version of *Miami Vice* was released in 2006, starring Colin Farrell as Crockett and James Foxx as Tubbs.
- Ricardo Tubbs, Crockett's crimefighting partner with the 'Rico Cooper' alias, was played by Philip Michael Thomas; Edward James Olmos was police chief Martin Castillo.

Midsomer Murders
Jaguar X-type, Rover 75

A 'whodunnit' mystery series in the best British traditions of Agatha Christie, *Midsomer Murders* has extended the TV popularity of its star John Nettles way beyond the instant recognition attained in his *Bergerac* days. At anything up to 102 minutes long, these well-executed dramas certainly give viewers plenty to get their teeth into, with little of the vulgarity that now pervades other primetime television. No doubt a younger audience, reared on the pap of reality shows and double-entendre-laden chatshows, finds *Midsomer Murders* staid, but the programme has proved a tremendously hot export property, loved by viewers from Northern Europe to South America, and even China.

The show follows the investigations of Chief Inspector Tom Barnaby, a character created by author Caroline Graham, who patrols Midsomer to probe away at the circumstances of the abnormal number of corpses littering that picturesque county. Nettles does a fine trade in knowing looks and disbelieving squints, and he's ably assisted by northerner Sergeant Gavin Troy (played by Daniel Casey, and now displaced by Sergeant Dan Scott, alias John Hopkins).

To get from village to village, of course, would be impractical on foot, so Barnaby has had a succession of saloon cars at his disposal, which have, since the show began in 1997 – nine series and 51 episodes ago – become progressively more exciting.

He began with a Ford Mondeo of the first generation, but this was ousted in 2000 by his new Rover 75. Troy's own slapdash driving style is constantly disdained by 'Sir'. The car's appearance in the show was an interesting example of 'product placement' by a Rover keen to gain exposure among well-heeled telly-addicts, and the British car seemed entirely appropriate to the attractive Home Counties scenery (mostly filmed in rural Buckinghamshire – prime Rover country) with its country lanes and gravel drives; it's not often Barnaby encounters a cadaver on a council estate...

Sadly, however, MG Rover was declared bankrupt in 2005, and the official receiver recalled all the company's cars out on loan for use in films and TV – some 72 vehicles, according to Peter Thompson of Rover's placement agency Hatched Brands, including over a dozen in Germany. That meant Barnaby lost his 75, although in real life John Nettles liked the car so much he

Lovely scenery, but murky goings-on

This show is filmed in the countryside outside London, in an arc from Surrey round to Essex, although the Bentley Productions crew is based at Pinewood Studios in Iver Heath, Buckinghamshire. Long Crendon is a much-used location, with a high street pleasingly free of concrete eyesores and chavs in tracksuits. Each episode costs a reassuringly expensive £1.3m to shoot, taking five weeks and a cast and crew of up to 120.

The show may have a genteel aura, but reveals some gruesome deaths involving farm machinery, decapitations, and stabbings. Sado-masochism and drugs have reared their ugly heads too, feeding the suspense of many a dark evening in the living rooms of Middle England.

bought a 75 Tourer estate for his own private use.

No matter, though: Jaguar was delighted to step into the breach for such a premium role, furnishing *Midsomer Murders* with a gleaming new X-type.

Minder

Jaguar XJ6, Daimler Double-Six, Ford Capri MKII

Arthur Daley is a character as vividly drawn as anything Charles Dickens could imagine, but viewers weren't entirely sure what they were getting when *Minder* was first broadcast on ITV on 29 October 1979. The entire network had just been on strike for 11 weeks, and the just-returned *TV Times* billed it vaguely as 'a thriller'.

Yet the show, about a prosperous but slippery used-car salesman, and the former jailbird he employs as his bodyguard (the Cockney word 'minder' wasn't widely known then) and general dogsbody, seemed to be infused with humour.

There was a magic to the casting, as the show paired *The Sweeney*'s action man, Dennis Waterman as minder Terry McCann, with comedy legend George Cole as his employer Daley. There was also something

special about the way it was filmed; just like *The Sweeney*. Thames TV's Euston Films shot the series almost entirely on location on London's streets, giving it a believable raw edge and bringing the characters – created by Leon Griffiths – to dodgy life. The stories revolve around the devious and cowardly Arthur being constantly rescued by Terry, and living in perpetual fear of his wife, never glimpsed and known only as "Er indoors."

Griffiths envisaged Arthur as a natural Jaguar driver in the original scripts. "Arthur could only ever have driven a Jaguar", he recalled. "It has always been the kind of car the people he admired aspired to." Hence, too, the Trilby hat, cigar and expensive overcoat.

Some 104 episodes of *Minder* were shot over a 15-year period, although from episode 70 Waterman departed the show and was replaced by Gary Webster playing Ray Daley who, as Arthur's nephew, occupied a similar role to Terry McCann.

Arthur's most notorious haunt is the Winchester Club, a seedy drinking den where the proprietor, Dave (Glynn Edwards), listens to Arthur's exploits with a mixture of sympathy and disbelief. However, Arthur's nerve centre is his used-car lot in west London. This really was a used-car lot, situated at the corner of

Daley's parade of dodgy motors

With a car lot at the centre of Arthur Daley's world in *Minder*, many cars are featured, although rarely new ones. In early episodes, he drives Jaguar XJ6 SIIs, a grey one registered 'SNV 696M' and a brown one 'TAN 488M'. Then follow several Daimler Double-Six SIIIs carrying numbers 'DYD 979V', 'E413 HKV' and 'G269 YLN'. One unusual Jag Arthur runs is a 1987 XJ40-style XJ6 3.6-litre. This silver car, registered 'D533 ERW', was loaned to Euston Films by Jaguar itself for series seven, after having served as a development prototype. It's now undergoing renovation by owner Mark Hardwick.

Terry McCann drove three Ford Capri MkIIs in *Minder*, including the 2.0S registered 'SLE 71R' seen in the show's opening credits for the first seven series; Arthur is on his forecourt trying to interest Terry in buying it, and they shake hands on the deal over the car's bonnet. In later episodes, Terry drives two newer Capris with the revised, post-1977 frontal styling; they carry numbers 'MJN 701V' and 'EUC 223V'.

Augustine Road and Dewhurst Road in Brook Green, London W14. But don't go looking for this iconic TV location; the gentrification of west London has seen new houses built on the site...

The Monkees
Pontiac GTO 'Monkeemobile'

The Monkees gained the unflattering nickname of the 'Pre-Fab Four', not because the band predated The Beatles, but because they were the total invention of US TV. Micky Dolenz, Mike Nesmith, Peter Tork (all American) and Davy Jones (British) were all working musicians when they auditioned for the parts; they kept their real names in the show. However, while they were filming, the show's music was often recorded by session musicians to save time. Of course, they were *inspired* by the Liverpudlian pop sensations. *The Monkees* was a zany comedy show about a four-piece band, created for NBC by Bob Rafelson and Bert Schneider. It first aired in September 1966 and ran for two seasons.

When two albums of *The Monkees* music were released, the TV show began to promote the records, rather than vice versa; the releases sold millions. The four actors then rehearsed the music themselves and did a concert tour of America, before recording the album *Headquarters*.

The 'Monkeemobile' was integral to the project from the start. It was designed by US customising legend Dean Jeffries, also a design consultant to MPC, makers of plastic model car kits. After Jeffries mentioned his new Universal assignment to George Toteff, MPC's CEO, Toteff contacted Pontiac's ad agency, McManus, John & Adams, and sealed a deal for Pontiac to supply the base car from which Jeffries could fashion the 'Monkeemobile'.

Pontiac delivered two GTO convertibles and Jeffries built two identical cars, one for filming and another for promotions, in just one month. The transformation was extreme. With its tall windscreen, a convertible top like a Ford Model T hot rod, a third row of seats in the bootspace, and radically altered front and rear styling, it was hard to spot the GTO underpinnings.

Pontiac was concerned its product had been made to look silly, but the cameras were already rolling before they could object. However, a promotional tie-up between *The Monkees*, Pontiac and Kellogg's proved wildly successful. George Toteff, meanwhile, sold an incredible 7 million 'Monkeemobile' model kits.

Hey, hey, they're the Monkeemobiles

The fate of the two 'Monkeemobiles' has been fully chronicled by America's *Pontiac Enthusiast Magazine*.

The first car, the only one used for filming, followed the four band members on a tour of Australia, but failed to be returned to the US, and instead ended up as a hotel courtesy car in Puerto Rico. It was sold in a bankruptcy sale on the island in May 1992 for just $5,000, because no-one seemed to know what it was! It's now in loving ownership in New York, and in remarkably good original condition.

The second car did the promotional rounds, including being modified to do wheel-stands at custom car events, before eventually being snapped up by film and TV car doyen George Barris. Until recently it was on permanent display at the Star Cars Museum in Gatlinburg, Tennessee, USA.

Mr Bean
Mini

Rowan Atkinson's passion for cars

Rowan Atkinson is a fast-car fanatic. He started his car collection in 1981 with an Aston Martin V8 after achieving stardom on the BBC2 sketch show *Not The Nine O'Clock News*. He soon added a Lancia Delta Integrale and Bentley Mulsanne Turbo. He then became one of the few owners of a McLaren F1, using some of the box office takings from the movie *Bean* to buy the £635,000, 240mph car. He is also the proud possessor of a Heavy Goods Vehicle driving licence.

However, Atkinson hit the headlines – and a Rover Metro – when he had an accident in the McLaren in 1999 at 30mph. It caused £100,000 of damage to the car. Then he also pranged his Aston Martin V8 Vantage Zagato at an Aston Martin Owners' Club competitive event in 2001. Nothing dents his enthusiasm, though – Rowan Atkinson even writes a column for that speed freak's monthly essential *Evo* magazine.

Thanks to the absence of virtually any dialogue – *Mr Bean* relies purely on visual humour – the programme has been astoundingly popular all over the world, making Atkinson's gurning face familiar to tens of millions.

However, it's surprising to remember that a mere 14 half-hour shows were made from 1989 to 1995, and that Atkinson, who came up with the concept with his screenwriting chum Richard Curtis, found it exhausting to make.

"I had fun thinking of the ideas, and it's fun looking at the takes, but that's really it", he told one interviewer. The feature film spin-off *Bean*, released in 1997, was a huge international hit, said to have netted Atkinson at least £11m, some of which he spent on motoring toys.

Rowan Atkinson's comic creation is a slapstick figure in the great tradition of Buster Keaton and Jacques Tati's Monsieur Hulot. He's both childishly selfish and entirely likeable, and as he makes his way through life, causing mayhem, he seems blissfully unaware of other people and their approach to life.

Quite how he's ever supposed to have passed his driving test is never made entirely clear, but Mr Bean is nonetheless proud to be a Mini owner. In the first ever episode of the show, he drives a red example, but from the third show onwards this is replaced by an apple-green example with a black bonnet. This car is another iconic vehicle that's found its way into the collection of Keswick's Cars Of The Stars Museum; it was acquired in 1997 after several years of touring the country for display at shows.

We first see Bean in the opening episode entitled, simply, *Mr Bean*. He drives to a school and, on the way, his red Mini has its first comic encounter with a light blue Reliant Regal Supervan III. The van gets tipped on its side in a skirmish, and the bumper-to-bumper battle between the Mini and the three-wheeler becomes a recurring feature throughout the remaining shows. The green car arrives in the third episode, *The Curse Of Mr Bean*. It is seen variously driven by him from an armchair strapped to the roof, or else from the back seat as he changes clothes. He later decides to uprate the car's locking system by fitting a large bolt and padlock to the driver's door.

Only Fools & Horses
Reliant Regal van, Ford Capri MKII

Many British TV-watchers know the Trotter family as well as their own. When *Only Fools & Horses* is aired, for half an hour every viewer is a drinker in 'The Nag's Head' in Peckham, listening to another of wideboy Derek Trotter's scams, or commiserating with the well-meaning Rodney. We know those quirky catchphrases, those mutually-dependent relationships, and the whole knock-off culture of Sarf London, as if we were slap-bang in the middle of it. You can thank the excellence of John Sullivan's writing for that.

What we don't seem to know, however, is our Reliants.

Trotter's Independent Trading Co, operating in New York, Paris and Peckham, uses a Reliant van for its low-rent business of selling dodgy goods on the local market. Moreover, it's a Reliant Regal van.

One or two vehicles get their names skewed in the popular conscience, and these contortions become permanent. For example, people always say "E-type Jaguar" or "8-litre Bentley" when the cars are actually the Jaguar E-type and Bentley 8-litre. "Robin Reliant" is another twisted semantic. It's Reliant Robin. But the marque name and model title are so closely linked that many

The Trotter family story

As the story ran for 22 years, it was inevitable the 'situation' in *Only Fools & Horses* would develop. The Trotters' father has vanished and their mum is dead, and the granddad who lived with them died in 1983 after the real death of actor Lennard Pearce. He was replaced by Uncle Albert, who was around until 1999 when that actor, Busty Merryfield, also passed away.

More importantly, each brother finds the woman of his dreams, which puts an extra strain on their relationship, and they both have children.

Derek eventually moves up in the world, leaving the driving of the Reliant to Rodney, and buying himself a Ford Capri MkII 3-litre Ghia, in lurid green with a black vinyl roof and a fake tigerskin-upholstered interior.

In 2005, John Sullivan devised a spin-off series called *The Green Green Grass*. In it, Boycie (played by John Challis), an obnoxious used-car salesman and old school pal of Del, moves his family from Peckham to rural Shropshire, to escape death threats from underworld hoods the Driscoll brothers. In his new situation, he drives a large American pick-up, but his wife Marlene (Sue Holderness) is a brassy fish-out-of-water in the countryside.

think it's a Robin in *Only Fools & Horses*. It's a Regal, for goodness sake – a Regal!

When the BBC sit-com first aired in 1981, the Reliant Regal had been obsolete for seven years. But being a three-wheeler, it continued to enjoy reduced road tax and, being made of plastic and having a tiny 700cc engine, it was very light and very frugal – making it a "lovely jubbly" choice, as Del would say, for the canny small businessman.

Opposite: Del Trotter, centre, with little brother Rodney, right, and their Uncle Albert, no doubt on their way to yet another business disaster.

How to understand Reliants

Reliant had been making three-wheeled vans since 1936, aimed at the small business that needed the lowest possible running costs. In fact, it only branched out into cars in 1952, when the Regal name was first used. The Regal 3/25 series (the figures stood for three wheels and 25bhp, the power output of the vehicle's 600cc engine) made its debut in 1962, and it's the van version of this model that Del and Rodney drive during so many of their capers.

It's easy to mock it, but this was a very successful vehicle; 105,824 of these Regal-type models were made, of which a large number were vans. The engine was uprated to 700cc in 1967. The BBC's special effects team gave the Reliant dramatic plumes of exhaust smoke and various traits of unreliability. In reality, these were generally reliable vehicles that could return up to 60mpg. As they were classed officially as tricycles, Reliant owners like the Trotters paid motorcycle-like levels of road tax, and they could also be driven on a motorbike licence. Oh, and by the way, it's a Reliant Regal not a Robin...

Like the Regal, *Only Fools & Horses* didn't look too promising; the story of two brothers, one a schemer and one a dreamer, living in a grotty tower block with their grandfather. But the brilliant comic performance of David Jason as 'Del-Boy' Trotter, and the hangdog acting skills of Nicholas Lyndhurst as his brother 'Rodders' – plus a dose of tear-jerking sentimentality – quickly turned it into a gem. Between 1981 and 1991, 57 shows were recorded, followed by seven one-off, feature-length Christmas specials up to 2003 that drew huge audiences of festive viewers.

In mainstream TV comedy terms, it doesn't get any bigger, and most of the scripts were genuinely hilarious. In a BBC poll in 2004, the show beat everything to become the nation's favourite sit-com, and with 24.3 million viewers, the 1996 three-part Christmas special has the biggest-ever ratings for a British sit-com. Still, like *Monty Python*'s 'dead parrot' sketch, some of the highlights – such as when Del falls off the end of the pub bar – are almost too familiar.

The Reliant van has become a star exhibit at the Cars Of The Stars Museum in Keswick, Cumbria, the extraordinary film and TV car collection built up by Peter Nelson. In grubby yellow paint, sporting a roofrack, and minus its hubcaps, it's absolutely 'as seen on TV'. The registration number is 'DHV 938D'. It has occasionally been hauled out of this comfortable retirement home for *Only Fools & Horses* Christmas specials. It has also inspired several replicas, driven by owners who evidently don't mind being noticed.

Opposite: A smoothie collects his lucky girl from the airport in an original Regal van.

Below: The Trotters' van in its most familiar territory – Peckham Market.

The Persuaders!

Ferrari Dino 246GT, Aston Martin DBS

Opposite: Lord Brett Sinclair, in suitably majestic surroundings, with his Bahama Yellow Aston Martin DBS.

Left: Sinclair and Danny Wilde debate the high life in Wilde's Ferrari Dino 246GT.

Once every possible ounce of small-screen value had been wrought from Simon Templar and his shiny-halo activities as *The Saint*, its producer Robert Baker set about creating a replacement show in 1970. He settled on a buddy-buddy format of two wealthy playboys, who spent their days lounging around on the French Riviera, and being roped into justice-seeking by a retired judge with files on villains he'd still dearly like to bring to book.

This scenario would have been too contrived for words had not the casting been so good. Roger Moore was already on-board, and he was allocated the part of Lord Brett Sinclair, a racy British aristocrat. But with the persuasive help of Lew Grade, Baker reeled in Hollywood legend Tony Curtis for the role of Danny Wilde, the financial equal of Sinclair, but a wise-cracking New Yorker who'd risen from nothing in the Bronx.

Freeze-frame at the ready

The complex intermix between location footage and studio-bound material shot at Pinewood resulted in the patchy continuity found in many ITC shows, and very much laid bare today by the DVD player and its freeze-frame button. One of the finest gaffes in *The Persuaders!* occurs when Sinclair's Aston overtakes a vehicle on what is supposed to be the French autoroute but is self-evidently a section of half-completed British motorway. As the car passes behind a truck, it's wearing its characteristic 'BS 1' number plates, only to emerge on the other side sporting the car's real registration number 'PPP 6H'.

Where are *The Persuaders!* cars now?

The status of the Ferrari Dino used in *The Persuaders!* is slightly mysterious. It seems the car Ferrari supplied was actually privately owned. Chassis number '00810', it was the 405th Dino built and was completed in May 1970. The first registered owner was Giovanni Cavedoni of Modena, according to Swiss Ferrari historian Marcel Massini, and the Dino still exists in Italy today after having changed hands several times.

With filming over, the Aston was sold through London dealer HR Owen and had five owners before *The Persuaders!* aficionado Mike Sanders bought it in 1994. "I liked the series and I bought it on a whim – it's a fun thing to have", he said. He then entrusted its painstaking restoration to Aston Martin at Newport Pagnell, and the company did such a stunning job that it's now recognised as possibly the finest six-cylinder DBS on the planet. It has a genuine 76,000 miles on the clock.

The two actors had an immediate rapport on-camera and off, and Curtis was particularly adept at ad-libbing to add charm to some hackneyed scripts which involved cartoonish bounders and unfeasibly glamorous distressed damsels, from Joan Collins to Kate O'Mara. It was light comedy-drama set against a gaudily exotic backdrop. In other words, perfect escapist TV.

Obviously, Baker well knew the value of having the right cars in the series. Aston Martin provided a six-cylinder DBS in Bahama yellow with a manual five-speed gearbox for Lord Sinclair, although the car was not quite what it seemed because it was, visually, to the same spec as the then-new DBS V8, with alloy wheels instead of wires. Ferrari furnished the producers with a red Dino 246GT, with the Modena registration number of '221400-MO', for Danny Wilde. The show's production supervisor, Johnny Goodman, personally picked the car up from Maranello and drove it straight round to the location set on the Cote d'Azur. Lucky man.

The cameras began rolling on *The Persuaders!* in June 1970, and the show was first broadcast in the autumn of 1971.

The opening episode *Overture* shows the two men, as yet unacquainted, racing the Aston and Ferrari against each other around the coast roads near Monaco; the footage is terrific and the backing track to the sequence, called *Gotta Get Away* and composed by Tony Hatch, is a groovy period piece...

Although these two cars appear in most episodes, Curtis and Moore also drive a variety of other vehicles, including Land Rovers, a Range Rover, a BMW 3.0S, a Mini Moke, Citroën H-type and Ford Econoline vans, and even an articulated petrol tanker.

Some driving sequences were shot in the Welsh mountains, often doubling for the hills in the south of France, while one scene in *Someone Like Me* sees Sinclair delivering his DBS to HR Owen's garage, on the A40 at Greenford, west London, for its service.

The episode *Someone Waiting* revolves around race-fixing in motor sport, with Lord

Sinclair driving his 'Sinclair Special' around Brands Hatch. The Sinclair character also features in the show's credits in a fake news cutting headlined 'Road news: Brett Sinclair enters Grand Prix'.

With a £2.5m budget, at the time *The Persuaders!* was the most expensive TV series ever filmed in the UK, each episode costing £80,000. But critics were not impressed. TC

Worsley, writing in the *Financial Times* in 1971, said: "If I had paid that sum and my writers came up with anything so childishly unconvincing as these stories I should want to know why."

While a massive hit worldwide, the show flopped badly in the US, where ABC scheduled it opposite CBS's *Mission: Impossible*. Just 24 hour-long shows were made, and plans for four more series were torn up.

Left: Danny Wilde, the Ferrari Dino, and a street in the south of France... and check out those groovy driving gloves.

The Prisoner
Lotus Seven, Mini Moke

The Prisoner became, a few years ago, too 'culty' by half. You can read any number of metaphors and conspiracies into its unusual scenario – a secret agent who's spirited away to a mysterious island village where 'they' try to extract from him his reasons for resigning. It's

A Seven for Number Six

The charisma of *The Prisoner* is powerful. The Lotus Seven's part in the series became legendary, so much so that – 25 years after it was made – Caterham Cars (which took over Seven manufacture from Lotus) launched a 'Prisoner' special edition, complete with yellow nose cone and dash-mounted plaque sporting the penny-farthing logo of the show. It was endorsed by Patrick McGoohan, who flew from California to launch the car at the 1990 Birmingham Motor Show. Forty were made, and McGoohan himself finally became a Seven owner when Nearn presented him with the keys to one of them – chassis No 6, obviously.

enigmatic and intriguing to watch. It's just that you may not want to hear about it from some wide-eyed, *Prisoner*-mad aficionado.

The Prisoner was the idea of Patrick McGoohan, who played the central 'prisoner' role of Number Six. The show's frenetic opening titles always repeat his capture sequence, and the episodes chart his single-minded determination to unmask his captors – particularly the God-like Number One – or else escape. "I am not a number," roars McGoohan, "I am a free man."

In the titles, Number Six drives a Lotus Seven Series II, a green car with a yellow nose-cone and registered 'KAR 120C'. It speeds straight towards the camera under gathering skies before Number Six drives to, and from, his resignation confrontation. The Seven's allusion to motoring freedom suited the central character of *The Prisoner*, but Number Six also divulges an interesting snippet in the episode *Many Happy Returns*. "I know every nut and bolt and cog," he growls. "I built it with my own hands!" Our man, it seems, constructed his own Lotus Seven kit...

McGoohan knew the value of 'casting' the right car. Possibly inspired by *The Avengers*, in 1965 he asked Lotus to loan an Elan for the show, but while visiting the Cheshunt factory,

he noticed the Seven and reckoned it had a more rebellious aura. Lotus happily obliged.

Later, the production team realised they'd need the Lotus back to shoot a scene in the final episode *Fall Out*. Unfortunately, 'KAR 120C' had been shipped to south America, so McGoohan begged Graham Nearn, of Lotus dealer Caterham Cars, to provide an identical replica. Nearn's workshop manager, David Wakefield, toiled overnight on the car, and Nearn drove it to the location in London the next day. While the shot was taken, Graham Nearn was further pressed into action as a film extra; he's seen in the show as a mechanic, cleaning the car and delivering the keys through Number Six's letterbox!

Another car makes a big impression in *The Prisoner*: the Mini Moke. Equipped with two-tone paintjobs and fringed Surrey tops, several serve as taxis in 'The Village', which is set in picturesque Portmeirion in north Wales. Mokes are excellent for filming because the actors are so clearly visible in them, but the cars also fitted the offbeat art direction of the show.

Opposite: Patrick McGoohan, left, Number Six in *The Prisoner*, and Caterham Cars founder Graham Nearn, with the iconic Lotus Seven.

Above: A Mini Moke on *The Prisoner* location set in Portmeirion.

The Professionals
Ford Capri, Escort & Granada, Nissan 200SX

Did you run around your school playground, pretending to be Bodie or Doyle, CI5 agents, holding your imaginary Browning pistol with two hands and shouting "Cover me!" to your crime-busting buddy? And did you yearn for a 3-litre Ford Capri so you could swing its rear end out like an alligator flicking its tail, depositing rubber on the road and tyre-smoke in the air?

Of course, if you have no idea what any of this is about, then possibly you were a responsible parent on the late 1970s, who never let your children watch the violent goings-on of *The Professionals* on a Saturday evening on ITV. Or, maybe, you're simply too young to have seen the show, often likened to a British *Starsky & Hutch*. You probably haven't caught it as a repeat, either; not on British terrestrial TV anyway, where Martin Shaw – who disliked his role as Ray Doyle, and is today familiar from *Judge John Deed* – has blocked re-runs since 1987. This is lamentable for fans, as *The Professionals* was widely enjoyed and fondly remembered.

The show revolves around the elite 'Criminal Intelligence 5' government agency, overseen by George Cowley (played, with dourness and ferocity, by Gordon Jackson), and his two finest operatives, Doyle, an ex-copper, and William Bodie (Lewis Collins), a

Rather more than just Capris

The chronology of cars used in *The Professionals* is tangled, despite the show being so firmly identified with the Ford Capri.

In the opening, 1977 season, the cars used were largely built, and supplied, by British Leyland. George Cowley was seen in a red Princess and a yellow Rover 3500 SD1; Bodie's character drove a white Triumph Dolomite Sprint and Doyle's a blue Triumph TR7 (plus a brown Rover 2000 P6 in a couple of stories).

For 1978, however, a wholesale switch to Ford saw boss man Cowley use the first of many Ford Granadas. A Capri, a highly unusual X-pack MkII 3.1-litre in silver, had appeared briefly in the first season in Doyle's hands, while Bodie had enjoyed a bronze 3.0-litre Ghia. For season two (1978), however, Bodie had a silver MkIII 3.0S, and two identical cars were used for filming. Doyle, meanwhile, was issued with a white Ford Escort RS2000 that he used in 1978- and 1979-season episodes. Both men used a variety of gold and silver Capri 3.0Ss in 1980 and 1981 and, curiously, sometimes also an old blue Triumph 2500 MkII saloon for undercover work.

Although the many Fords used in *The Professionals* were returned to the manufacturer, and eventually sold on as everyday used cars, almost all of them have been tracked down and are now owned by fans of the series, and most are in fine fettle.

CI5: The New Professionals

The concept for the show was dusted off in 1998 for *CI5: The New Professionals*, which ran to 13 episodes and was shot by David Wickes Television on location in the UK, the USA and South Africa.

None of the original cast reappeared (Gordon Jackson had died in 1990), although Brian Clemens and Laurie Johnson were both involved. CI5 was now an international organisation that was just as likely to be called in to combat ivory poachers as gun-toting madmen. The 'Cowley' role was taken by Edward Woodward as Harry Malone, while his top operatives now numbered three: Sam Curtis (the Brit actor Colin Wells), Chris Keel (Canadian Kal Weber) and Tina Backus (Lexa Doig, another Canadian).

A raft of new car stars were drafted in. This was led by the tail-happy Nissan 200SX taking on the Capri mantle, but other cars featured included a Nissan Terrano, Lotus Esprit, Ford Mondeo and Range Rover.

It was shown in the UK on satellite channel Sky One, but the revival wasn't a success.

former SAS tough nut. The two chaps are a pair of politically-incorrect womanisers, given the chance, while their special status means fast cars are genuine tools of their trade, and they're driven to near-destruction in the pursuit – literally – of everyone from terrorists to racial supremacists. Doyle is the compassionate, if hot-headed, one, Bodie more vicious but also more tactical.

Created by Brian Clemens and made by his company for London Weekend Television, 57 hour-long episodes of *The Professionals* were produced between 1977 and 1981, in five series, although unseen shows were still being aired as late as 1983. It is, as the genre has evolved, 'bloke TV' par excellence, with the fact that the programme was condemned at the time for its violence, laddishness and lairy driving, all building mystique. Seen on video today. though, its misdemeanours seem mild – there's pretty tame swearing, precious little gore, and several stories that touch raw nerves and should, therefore, have been applauded. The Bodie/Doyle banter is entertaining. And the action, which was often filmed on London's streets, seems impossibly realistic by today's anodyne standards.

After the first series in 1977, the producers – who included Laurie Johnson, composer of that rousing theme music – made several changes. The title sequence was altered, from one showing a Rolls-Royce Silver Shadow barreling into view before a CI5 operative tackles an assault course, to a faster-paced montage of the three stars. It opens with an

iconic TV moment – a dark blue Ford Granada MkI bursting through a plate glass window. This gives the impression of diving from an upper-storey window, but Brian Clemens reveals that what you see on screen is actually a reflection in glass of what happened opposite; "so that you could really appreciate the car dip", he adds.

Another change was the removal from the characters of their British Leyland cars, which included a Princess, Rover SD1, Triumph TR7 and Triumph Dolomite, and the substitution of Ford cars throughout. This reflected growing resentment from Clemens and his colleagues at British Leyland's grudging co-operation and the terrible reliability of its products, plus the eagerness of Ford to jump on board what was an instant success. "Also, as a writer, you learn from mistakes", says Clemens. "We definitely wanted to 'bulk up' the imagery of the characters." And the wheel-spinning Capris and Escort RS2000s Ford provided certainly gave Bodie and Doyle more on-screen grit, even if Martin Shaw might have deplored the added focus given to 'hardware' at the expense of acting ability. Ironically, although their on-screen driving appeared fast and furious, it was a stipulation that Collins and Shaw were always driven to the set...

The Protectors

Jensen Interceptor, Citroën SM *et al*

The Protectors was the perfect slice of jet-setting, super-stylish, car-filled hokum to enliven a Sunday tea-time in 1972.

The reason the show, which ran to 52 half-hour episodes, is so choc-full of great classic metal is probably down to a publicist called Gethin Bradley. He agreed to supply a Jensen Interceptor to be driven on-screen by the show's star Robert Vaughn, and told all his motoring PR chums about the show, who all decided to offer their wares too. Producer Gerry Anderson recently recalled the first day of filming.

"I turned up at Elstree to find the car park crammed full of brand new cars. The manufacturers just delivered them all because they'd heard we were making the show. I admired that – this was go-ahead stuff, really American! In the end, we 'cast' the cars for each script, rather like we did the actors..."

One of the most extraordinary car scenes occurs when a bright yellow Minijem (good guys) is chasing a Rover 2000 (bad) through the streets of London in the second series episode *Petard*; as the Rover is cornered, the Minijem mounts a low kerb, and its bonnet flies open and smashes the windscreen. This was clearly not supposed to happen.

However, the episode *Wheels* must have delighted Ford. It was based around the ludicrous notion of using a rally car to head off criminals by taking the forest route, while the bad guys stuck to the roads in a sinister black Merc. It turned into a thrilling promotional film about how to expertly handle a full rally-spec Escort Mk1 RS1600 – great stuff. But the storyline, like the car itself, does get pushed sideways somewhat.

Ritzy private detectives *The Protectors* were dreamed up by 66-year-old Sir Lew Grade himself. That perhaps explains why the central protagonist, Harry Rule, played by a 40-year-old Vaughn, seems absurdly middle-aged for a so-called action man, and also why he was teamed with 32-year-old Nyree Dawn Porter, whom Grade collared at an awards ceremony and cast on the spot as the widowed, English-born Italian contessa, Caroline di Contini. Grade then handed the whole project to puppet king Gerry Anderson. It was, in fact, a poisoned chalice.

Anderson added handsome Parisian techno-freak Paul Buchet (Tony Anholt) to the mix, but was soon at loggerheads with his Jensen-, Mustang-, Merc 280SL- and Volvo P1800ES-driving leading man Vaughn. "The crew may have thought I was all right to work

Famous Fiat was on a roll

The opening credits are collated from a sequence of shots culled from various sources, intermixed with footage establishing *The Protectors* as high-rolling action figures. Included is the helicopter sequence borrowed from the James Bond film *From Russia With Love,* and remarkable shots of a pale yellow Fiat 850 Coupé caught turning turtle. This is actually an out-take from an episode of *The Saint*, called *The Desperate Diplomat* and filmed in 1968, where Roger Moore's stunt double, Les Crawford, accidentally loses control of the tail-happy car.

with, but Gerry Anderson didn't like me at all", said Vaughn afterwards. "Nor did I like him." But it can't have helped the relationship when Robert Vaughn went on record as describing *The Protectors* as "tasteless junk"... while it was still being aired.

This was highly ironic because the one episode Vaughn himself directed, *It Could Be Practically Anywhere On The Island,* was later described by Grade himself as "a disaster, the worst episode I've ever seen of *anything*."

Opposite: Harry Rule aboard his Jensen Interceptor.

Above, left: The distinctive Interceptor shape.

Above, right: The Contessa Di Contini and Citroën SM.

Randall & Hopkirk (Deceased)

Vauxhall Victor, Austin Mini, Mercedes-Benz 280CE

In the opening episode of this quirky, supernatural series, which aired on ITV on 21 September 1969, one of the two main characters is run over outside his flat in London's Maida Vale. The car that knocks him down and kills him is a Humber Super Snipe. Not an auspicious beginning to a show about two private detectives, but it doesn't matter: his partner Jeff Randall is more than surprised when Marty Hopkirk returns – as a ghost.

As an ethereal presence in a crisp white suit who can do nothing physical, Marty is nonetheless a tremendous help – and often a lifesaver – for Jeff, because he can take himself anywhere at any time. And the dishevelled Jeff is the only person who can see or talk to the ever-anxious Marty. So Jeff keeps his bizarre new partnership secret – even from Marty's grieving widow Jeannie, now Jeff's partner in the detective agency – in case people think he's barmy.

The Randall & Hopkirk detective agency has never been prosperous, though. It's perpetually short of work, its office is austere,

and Jeff is a shambling mess in his trenchcoat. This extends to his car, too, a white, four-year-old Vauxhall Victor FD, registered 'RXD 996F'. The Victor was loaned by Vauxhall Motors' press fleet, but it's believed to have been scrapped in 1976.

For the time, this would've been the epitome of ordinary saloons, perfectly anonymous for a private dick, although the perennially single Jeff could have run something more economical. Like, for example, Marty's red Austin Mini, registered 'BAP 245B', that becomes Jean's car after his death. When Jeff drives this car, Marty constantly admonishes him for treating it roughly.

Only one, 26-episode series of *Randall & Hopkirk (Deceased)* was made. Its special effects were rudimentary (actors were commanded to freeze while Marty arrived or departed, and the film cut afterwards), and critics panned it. Its viewing figures were also disappointing to ATV-ITC. However, its imaginative premise, haunting musical score, and vivid performances, remained strong in the public's memory, so much so that it was remade in 2000 by the BBC, and promptly drew an audience of 10 million viewers. Love it or hate it, *Randall & Hopkirk (Deceased)* is a gold-plated cult classic.

A show with a ghost of a chance

Jeff Randall was brought to life by actor Mike Pratt, and Marty Hopkirk was played by Kenneth Cope. Irish comedian Dave Allen was considered for the role of Randall, but the on-screen rapport between Pratt and Cope was obvious at auditions. Cope, though, was forced to wear a very obvious wig throughout. The part of Jeannie Hopkirk went to Australian actress Annette Andre. Pratt's career ended tragically when he died of cancer in 1976. However, Cope still works in TV today, enjoying a long stint in soap *Brookside*.

The BBC raised *Randall & Hopkirk (Deceased)* from its own grave in 2000, and made two series of seven episodes, with comedians Vic Reeves and Bob Mortimer as, respectively, Marty and Jeff. Emilia Fox was the new Jeannie. The first series was written, produced and mostly directed by Charlie Higson, late of *The Fast Show,* and was a critical, as well as a ratings, hit. In the remake, Marty's old car passes to Jeff, and this time it's a gold Mercedes-Benz 280CE registered 'PYY 875Y'. As in the original, Marty scolds Jeff for driving it clumsily. A new character is played by Tom Baker as Marty's mentor; the Vauxhall connection in the 1969 show is saluted by naming this fellow ghost Wyvern.

Opposite: From left; Jeannie, Marty, Jeff, and guest damsel Laura, in a scene from the show.

Above: This gold Mercedes-Benz 280CE was used in the remake.

Left: A grave Jeff Randall in his Victor.

Roland Rat
Ford Anglia 100E

Can it really be true that a self-centred glove puppet with an annoying habit of saying "Yeah!" could have saved an entire television station?

Well, apparently, yes. The novel ITV breakfast station TV-AM had been launched to great fanfare in 1982 but, within a year, its ratings had slumped to just 100,000. Chief executive Greg Dyke took the decision to introduce *Roland Rat Superstar* as part of his fightback campaign, and something about the showbiz-loving, sunglasses-wearing little fella caught the British public's imagination. Within a couple of months, 1.8 million people were getting up and tuning in to his antics, aided and abetted by Roland's PA, Kevin The Gerbil ("number one Ratfan"), techno-geek Errol The Hamster, and Roland's tearaway young brother Little Reggie.

Roland was a good-natured and enthusiastic fame-chaser, perhaps reflecting the best aspects of the many celebrities who were interviewed plugging their books, films and records in TV-AM's dazzlingly-lit set at its Camden studio complex. These folk were used to the limousine lifestyle, but Roland still had some way to go on the wheels front.

His means of transport was the Ratmobile, a Ford Anglia 100E, heavily customised with spoilers and a huge bonnet bulge, and finished in shocking pink by Kevin. He bought the car for £85 in order to tour the UK, but it frequently broke down. In this naff-looking contraption, Roland and the gang are seen, among other escapades, rescuing Glenis The Guineapig from the pets department at Harrods for a dubious new life as Roland's adoring girlfriend.

"There's nothing like a Rolls-Royce", Roland declares in the Ratmobile, "and this is nothing like a Rolls-Royce!"

Roland and his rodent retinue were introduced on TV-AM by Michael Parkinson, on 19 March 1983, from a shed on top of the TV-AM building. As the show's viewing figures – presumably bolstered by mothers with children – snowballed, he was featured regularly, both live in the studio (via "Shedvision") and in many filmed inserts. But

Rat *joins* sinking ship

Roland Rat was created, operated and voiced by David Claridge, a highly experienced puppeteer, who had previously come up with the Mooncat puppet character for ITV's children's show *Get Up And Go!* He had also provided puppets for the BBC2 alternative sit-com *The Young Ones* in 1982, and 10 years later he created Brian The Dinosaur for the Saturday morning kids' show *Parallel 9.*

As well as the pink Ford, Claridge had full character backgrounds for Roland and his scuttling pals. Roland, for instance, was born in the sewers under King's Cross station, and had ambitions to own homes around the globe and get himself a knighthood; Kevin was born in Leeds under the star sign Gemini; and the Welsh Errol collected leeks and, unsurprisingly, liked vegetarian cooking.

eventually the ratpack moved on, shifting to the BBC in 1985, where two series of *Roland Rat: The Series* were made for primetime Saturday night airing, featuring new characters such as Roland's pet flea Colin. Since then, the ever-cheerful Roland has popped his snout up periodically in the TV schedules across all terrestrial channels, uttering those dreaded words: "I'm wonderful, I'm marvellous – yeah!"

Opposite: Roland Rat in his Ratmobile.

Left: He may have been irritating but kids loved him – oh, and he 'saved' TV-AM.

Saber of London
Porsche 356

"Good evening", said the impeccably spoken, one-armed actor Donald Gray; "I'm Mark Saber, and this is London." Then the action got underway, as Saber, a former Scotland Yard detective turned private sleuth, unravelled another perplexing case. Between autumn 1955 and spring 1959, Donald Gray – who lost his arm during World War Two – sleuthed his way through an incredible 156 half-hour shows, in five series known variously as *Mark Saber*,

Saber of London and *The Vise*. Surely no TV artist worked harder; two instalments were filmed each week.

For behind *Mark Saber* was a phenomenon that surely defines the term 'television industry'. American brothers Edward and Harry Lee Danziger produced over 350 half-hour TV shows and some 60 B-movies between 1955 and 1961. Their New Elstree Studios, converted from a Hertfordshire aero-engine

plant, was a veritable film factory, churning out its routine fare at a hectic pace.

Although born in South Africa, Gray's upper-class diction had made him a BBC announcer before he took the Saber role, and he was a decent actor despite the series once being derided as "the corniest show on TV."

How could it not be? The Danzigers' penny-pinching methods were legendary. They would scavenge sets from other movies and then get their scriptwriters to create stories around them. Actors received a pittance, and were often hired just by phoning the Danzigers – no matter what the role. And everyone involved, from the directors down, was urged to get each show, or film, completed as rapidly as possible and move on to the next one...

Mark Saber was the Danzigers' flagship, popular in the US, and Donald Gray made enough money from its first two series to buy himself a new Porsche 356 cabriolet. Typically, his own car was pressed into service for filming from series three onwards! Previously, almost everything he'd driven on-screen had been a mundane saloon.

The Danzigers low-budget *modus operandi* endured on shows like *Man From Interpol* and *Richard The Lionheart* until 1961, when they closed their studios and moved into owning

One-armed and dangerous

Mark Saber outings are rare on DVD and TV (Bravo was its last home in the early 1990s). Some shows are missing from the archives and Danziger authority David Moore (his impressive website is at www.78rpm.co.uk), has dedicated himself to tracking down all the lost episodes. However, these are his picks for the best show in each series.

- Series 1: *Hear No Evil* – Brian Clemens' tale of an old lady in danger from her relatives.
- Series 2: *A Hatful of Trouble* – a girl thinks her stepmother is a spy.
- Series 3: *Six Months to Talk* – a cracking mystery.
- Series 4: *Death Hides Out* – another old lady, this time haunted by a ghost.
- Series 5: *Kill and Run* – excellent study of a femme fatale.

Donald Gray had several assistants throughout the series, often played by American actors. His sidekick in series four was played by Robert Arden. Shortly before he died in 2005, aged 82, he vividly recalled Gray's Porsche – and driving style.

"Donald Gray was a pleasure to work with, and not a jealous actor. A gentleman in every sense of the word. But a scary driver. We'd do some scenes in the Porsche, and my heart would sometimes be sitting in my mouth as, at speed, he would change gear with his one arm – no hand on the wheel – controlling the car with his knee. I still break out in a sweat when I think of it."

hotels and cinemas. Poor old Donald Gray, however, found himself so utterly typecast by *Mark Saber* that he made few acting appearances again, with the notable exception of voicing Colonel White in Gerry Anderson's puppet classic *Captain Scarlet*. He died in 1978. Wonder what became of 'TGP 668'?

The Saint &
Return of the Saint
Volvo P1800, Jaguar XJ-S

NUV 647E

By the time the cameras wrapped on the last of 118 episodes of *The Saint* at Elstree Studios in the summer of 1968, the show and its star, Roger Moore, had propelled the Volvo P1800 to instant worldwide recognition.

The Saint, the nickname for Simon Templar, a latterday Robin Hood created by novelist Leslie Charteris in the 1920s, had already been the subject of radio serials and movies when British film producers Robert Baker and Monty Berman turned him into a TV series. They had specialised in reasonably successful if lurid horror flicks. *The Saint*, though, was to be a slick production of one-hour contemporary adventures. Charteris sold them the rights, Lew Grade's ATV-ITC organisation provided the backing, and a handsome young actor called Roger Moore was cast in the lead role.

In the books, Templar drove powerful, imaginary vintage roadsters called Hirondels or Furillacs, but for the TV series, he needed something real and eye-catching.

It's often said that Volvo supplied the P1800 for free. In fact, ITC paid for it like any other customer. It was in bright white and registered '71 DXC'. Driven straight to the studio, it was featured in the very first episode, *The Talented Husband*, given fake 'ST 1' number plates (this registration number was never owned by ITC),

A happy accident, thanks to Jaguar

The Saint Volvo phenomenon is an accident; a Volvo should never have been in the show at all. The producers wanted a Jaguar, but were rebuffed by the Coventry carmaker. "When we geared up for the series in 1962, I tried every conceivable car company to get a car for the show", recalled Johnny Goodman, the production supervisor. "At that time no-one seemed to appreciate the incredible free publicity they would derive from their car appearing on TV week after week."

Roger Moore intended to buy a new car himself, and offered to let the production company use it for filming too. He wanted a Jaguar Mk10, then very new and super-cool – an E-type would, in fact, have been difficult for this tall man to negotiate on set. Yet Jaguar flatly refused to push the young star to the top of the waiting list.

"In the end, a buddy of mine mentioned he'd seen a new and rather exotic sports car called a Volvo driving around town. I'd never even heard of it. Anyway, I sent Roger down to the showroom to take a look." A legend was created.

So Grade instead syndicated *The Saint* to small TV stations across America as a late-night schedule filler. Thanks to dogged TV nightowls, within two years it was a cult hit. Moreover, Volvo was amazed at the publicity its car generated on TV. In 1963, it launched a revised P1800S model, and to get the latest version into the show, the company provided an example to ITC, registered '77 GYL'. Roger Moore enjoyed the 'perk' of using the car at the weekends.

In the USA, *The Saint* was getting big local ratings. NBC wasn't too proud to reconsider the show, and the opportunity came at 11pm one Saturday in 1965. Viewers loved it and NBC's figures zoomed. It wasn't a freak, either: the same thing happened six weeks on the trot, boosted by reviewers who liked this quirky show from London, England with its immaculately attired, mannered and principled leading man.

NBC snapped up all 71 black-and-white episodes produced so far, and pressed Grade for more shot in colour. Robert Baker and Roger Moore formed a new company to make the shows, and Elstree hummed as 47 more episodes were churned out.

Volvo was delighted too. For these programmes, it provided two more P1800Ss in their very latest spec, 'NUV 647E' and 'NUV 648E'. They were shod with Minilite magnesium wheels to better fill the otherwise gaping wheelarches, and given extra spotlamps to make the obligatory car chases appear even more dramatic.

Above: This Volvo P1900 was the first of several cars to be used in *The Saint* by Simon Templar.

Opposite page: Templar returned in 1978 portrayed by a different actor and driving this white Jaguar XJ-S.

and quickly became as integral to Templar's on-screen persona as his sharply-tailored suit. Volvo also supplied additional components so a mock-up of the car's interior could be built at Elstree.

Lew Grade took *The Saint* showreels to New York in 1963, confident the big networks would want it. He got a nasty shock. At the screening of an episode for Mort Werner, vice-chairman of NBC, the programme stopped at what would, on TV, be the first ad break. Werner broke the silence: "Lew, I've never seen so much crap in all my life." Rival networks weren't enamoured either.

The Saint is still screened on cable channels. It's made a vast amount of profit, and was primarily responsible for ATV winning two Queen's Awards for Export in 1968 and '69.

'NUV 648E' had a string of subsequent owners, but by 1994 it had been acquired by Peter Nelson for his Cars of the Stars collection in Keswick, Cumbria. Bill Krzastek was prepared for disappointment when, in October 2004, he tentatively asked Nelson if he would consider selling it. But as Nelson also owns the earlier Saint Volvo '77 GYL' (no-one knows what became of 'NUV 647E' or '71 DXC'), he said "yes". Krzastek subsequently spent a small fortune restoring the careworn car in the UK, before shipping it home to his native Virginia, USA.

Bill first saw the car he now owns on 17 February 1968. It was his 16th birthday, and the episode shown (the 100th made) remains his favourite: Invitation to Danger was directed by Moore and stars Shirley Eaton. "The car is used more extensively in it than any other episode, and is even driven by Ms Eaton, so it wins hands down." To prove he's kept some objectivity, he says The Master Plan episode is "a really terrible one."

The halo gets a re-polish

In 1978, Simon Templar was back in Return Of The Saint. This time, he was played by Ian Ogilvy... and Jaguar fell over itself to help, providing two white XJ-Ss for filming which, this time, included weeks of location work in France and Italy. One was actually the 17th XJ-S built, in 1975, a factory demonstrator with the rare fitment of a sunroof and manual gearbox. Ogilvy loved driving it, and asked if he could drive it back to England after filming finished in Rome. He got as far as Florence before he'd burned the clutch out. The car was last heard of offered on eBay in 2003, where bids failed to hit the mystery vendor's reserve.

The Secret Service
Ford Model T

Until the recent Network DVD release of *The Secret Service*, this charming little series had been a lost gem of British TV history. It's highly unusual, in that it mixes the 'Supermarionation' puppet techniques, perfected by Gerry Anderson, with live action. There's something else weird about it – at least, it must have felt pretty weird to its star, the tongue-twisting comedian Stanley Unwin. He plays Father Stanley Unwin, but appears in close-up only once in the opening titles. The rest of the time, he voices an astonishingly life-like puppet model

of himself... with occasional outbursts of his famous 'Unwinese' gobbledegook language.

In an unlikely follow-up to *Stingray*, *Thunderbirds* and *Captain Scarlet & The Mysterons*, *The Secret Service* has Father Unwin working incognito for BISHOP, British Intelligence Secret Headquarters, Operation Priest, and in charge of fellow agent Matthew, who works undercover as the Reverend's gardener. Using a special device concealed inside a bible, Unwin is able to shrink Matthew to a third of his normal size,

and carry him around in a custom-made suitcase, so that he can be sent on otherwise impossible missions.

Father Unwin has his own, archaic-looking car, called Gabriel. It's a 1917 Ford Model T roadster, shown bearing the registration number 'T 42'. In one episode, *More Haste, Less Speed*, it too is shrunk in size.

This 66% reduction was essential to the show. The puppets and their sets were all two-thirds smaller than in real life, and these scenes were carefully inter-cut with live action segments where all people were seen either in long-shot or obscured. This meant that large savings on model-making time and costs could be made when, for example, all that was needed was a shot of Father Unwin pulling into his garage in the Model T.

Obviously, you can usually tell a puppet set from a real location but, sometimes it's not easy, and the series exudes such charm and incredible, loving craftsmanship in all its detail, that viewers – whether children or adults – soon just enjoy the plots, as the unassuming vicar brings a variety of fiendish security risks to book. And the show features plenty of the spectacular, miniaturised disasters for which Anderson's special effects team became deservedly renowned.

The savage Grade and the wonderful Gabriel

Why has *The Secret Service* remained so obscure, when Gerry Anderson shows have such a massive following? The answer to that is in the show's fate. When Anderson screened it to Lew Grade, the cigar-chomping TV mogul was horrified when Unwin started talking in his nonsensical language – which, itself, was part of the show, because he used it as his bumbling cover. Grade thought that viewers in the US, his key sales territory for any ITC-backed show, wouldn't be able to understand it and would be put off. Despite Anderson's protests, the show was cancelled on the spot after only 13 half-hour episodes had been filmed. Grade's disenchantment meant that *The Secret Service* was barely shown on ITV in Britain either, so the 2005 DVD release means it's pretty much a brand new show for many Anderson fanatics.

The Ford Model T used in the show was renovated and repainted in black and yellow by Gerry Anderson's production team. "We thought we would make it look prettier", he recalls. It was also given the tongue-in-cheek name of Gabriel, which was painted in black on the bodysides. Its maximum speed was 40mph, although British Intelligence was supposed to have upped that – to a startling 50mph! Stanley Unwin did all the driving on-screen in character.

An exact one-third-size scale model of the distinctive Model T was built by Space Models for the puppet scenes. "It was an absolutely wonderful model, beautifully made and radio-controlled", recalls Anderson. "It cost a fortune and, if it had crashed while being radio-controlled, it would have been expensive to repair and, of course, the filming would have had to stop. Fortunately, that never happened."

Starsky & Hutch

Ford Gran Torino

Well, here it is – for many people, the ultimate 'TV car'. When the first series of *Starsky & Hutch* was broadcast on America's ABC network, beginning on 10 September 1975, the switchboard of Spelling Goldberg Productions in Beverly Hills was jammed with calls from people wanting to know what the car was, whether Starsky drove it home at night, and where they could get one. Of course, it was largely a standard production model, but the way the producers had dressed it up for filming caused a sensation.

Creator William Blinn planned *Starsky & Hutch* to be unlike the routine cop shows then populating US TV. Dave Starsky and Ken 'Hutch' Hutchinson are two plain-clothes detectives at work on the streets of the fictional Bay City, California (for which, read San Francisco), but they are also good friends who help each other to do whatever's necessary to get their guys.

They were funny, they respected each other's foibles, and they used their savvy on one of the toughest police beats anywhere in the US. They were also jolly good-looking. Starsky, the swarthy hunk, was played by Broadway actor Paul Michael Glaser, and Hutch, the clean-cut blond surf bum, enacted by ex-singer/songwriter showbiz all-rounder David Soul. Starsky was the rough diamond, Hutch the well-educated middle-class boy, but both were devoted to their police work. These were the first TV detectives to appear on teenaged girls' bedroom walls.

Opposite: Starsky's "tomato" in action – an estimated 90 cars were crashed during the punishing shooting schedule.

Above: Starsky (left) and Hutch, TVs first pin-up cops.

A classic in the making

Ford was dead chuffed with the attention its otherwise unfashionable mid-size coupé received in *Starsky & Hutch*; it was deluged with requests for replicas, and it seemed churlish to refuse. So, in spring 1976, 1000 special-edition *Starsky & Hutch* Gran Torinos rolled off its Chicago production line.

They were painted red, of course, and featured that all-important white stripe (although differing slightly from the one on the actual TV cars). They have since become highly collectable cultural icons; as templates are available to add that desirable stripe to any old Gran Torino, though, checking the Vehicle Identification Number against factory records is the only way to avoid snaring a fake. In homage, Ford UK built a Starsky & Hutch lookalike for the 1977 Motorfair... based on a humble Cortina.

The Torino itself was introduced in 1968 to replace the Fairlane, both cars being 'mid-size' in US parlance, but still enormous by European standards. The complex range culminated in the Gran Torino notchback coupé used in *Starsky & Hutch*, a V8-powered muscle car that was actually discontinued after 1976.

Starsky & Hutch made great viewing when it was new in the late-1970s, and today is recognised as probably the best and certainly most charismatic cop show to come out of America during that era.

However, at first, it wasn't ideal family viewing. Particularly in the opening two seasons, the stories were gritty and often pretty violent. Media criticism led Spelling-Goldberg's team of hard-working writers to tone down the toughness from 1977 onwards, although they did an admirable job of keeping the show's streetwise feel. This freed up more screen space to develop the romantic sides of the two bachelor cops' characters, leading to longer rehearsals, but it also led to a gradual fall-off in viewing figures as the mush factor grew, which culminated in the show being axed in 1979.

However, the affection for *Starsky & Hutch* was such that a movie version was filmed in 2004. It starred Ben Stiller as Starsky and Owen Wilson as Hutch, and was uprooted to the 21st century. Producers decided not to tamper with the Gran Torino, though – the genuine 1976 article rode again, complete with white stripe. The film was well-received.

Typical of their whatever-it-takes methods is their friendship with Huggy Bear (Antonio Fargas), an underworld informant and hustler from New York, although their relationship with him – and much else about their methods – is frowned upon by brooding police chief Captain Harold Dobey (Bernie Hamilton).

Starsky is actually portrayed as something of a car nut over his Ford Gran Torino, which gets far more screen time than Hutch's nondescript and scruffy 1973 Ford Galaxie. The 1975- (later 1976-) model Torino is the duo's main means of giving chase. The car's distinctive livery of red bodywork with a white, 'Nike'-like 'swoosh' stripe along the flank was apparently created at the suggestion of producer Aaron Spelling.

He is supposed to have said to George Granier, transportation chief for Spelling-Goldberg Productions: "George, we need a specialty car for a new series. Do something to one of our cars to make it stand out." Initial ideas were for a Chevrolet Camaro in green and white, but Chevrolet couldn't supply the right car. So the distinctive, pointed white stripe was added to a specially-painted red Torino, and swept up and over its roof. It also gained a set of fat, five-slot 'kidney bean' alloy wheels, and jacked-up suspension. It becomes Hutch's running joke that the machine his buddy lavishes so much time on is referred to as "the tomato".

The cars used in the show – and there were around a dozen, variously for static shots, driving scenes and stunts – came from Ford's Studio-TV Car Loan Program. Much of the early car-chase driving was done by Chuck Picerni, the show's stunt co-ordinator. A novelty was the use of a roof-mounted camera so viewers could feel the sensation of the Torino tearing through Bay City's streets, and could also see Starsky's nifty, clip-on roof beacon flashing away merrily. The car's own radio call-sign was "Zebra Three".

Some estimates reckon that, on average, one Torino was crashed for each show made. Not surprising, really, as the schedule was brutal: each one was shot in seven days, four days on location and three in the studio. And they churned them out; there were four series of *Starsky & Hutch* between 1975 and 1979, a total of 89 hour-long shows, together with the 90-minute pilot episode. The series started airing on BBC1 in the UK on 30 April 1976. The constant gaffe running throughout is the noise Starsky's Gran Torino makes; the cars used were automatics, yet the soundtrack signifies a distinctly manual gearshift...

Opposite: Ford dressed this Cortina up to look like Starsky's Torino, to the delight of British motor show visitors.

Supercar
Supercar

One of those questions that devotees of expensive cars love to argue over is: "What was the first supercar?" Was it the mid-engined Lamborghini Miura or De Tomaso Mangusta of 1966, or maybe the handsome, front-engined Ferrari Daytona of a couple of years later? These exotics came close, of course, but the word first appeared in 1960 heralding the fourth of Gerry Anderson's increasingly sophisticated puppet shows for children and, secretly, adults too.

The 'supercar' in *Supercar* is a futuristic and gadget-packed hybrid of car, rocket, plane and boat, operating out of a secret base at Black Rock in the Nevada desert. Designed for rescue missions wherever they may be called for – from the ocean floor to outer space, Supercar is often seen battling arch-enemy Masterspy, who would dearly like to get his mitts on it. Supercar was about 25ft long and capable of 1500mph – beat that, Lamborghini!

Its engines could spin to 15,000rpm before a rocket-fired vertical take-off through the opened roof of the Nevada hangar. Once shooting upwards, its retractable wings could be unfolded, and it could be flown like a plane. Unlike conventional cars, though, it didn't have wheels to travel along the roads, as it was able to hover just above the road surface, while naturally there was an on-board screen to present a view through bad weather, a periscope for underwater excursions, and an ejector seat in case of total, pear-shaped, malfunction.

At the controls of this awesome machine sat Mike Mercury, your standard-issue, jut-jawed hero, albeit one with strings rising from his head and limbs. His 'craft' was the creation of two scientists, Professor Popkiss and Dr Beaker, although in real life it was designed and built by art director Reg Hill. It was made of wood at a cost of about £1,000, and was painted red, yellow, grey and blue – although, because the 39-episode show was shot in black-and-white, you'd never have known. The studio model measured 7ft long.

Of course, this was all kids' stuff, designed for teatime consumption by young children in the days when space travel and exploration was in its exciting infancy. But many of the

Did Ford inspire Supercar?

Designer Reg Hill would have had plenty of rocket-like concept cars from which to draw inspiration – they were regularly displayed by US manufacturers Ford, General Motors and Chrysler during the 1950s, each trying to out-do the others for outrageousness and implausibility.

The closest to the Supercar design appears to be Ford's be-finned extravaganza, the FX-Atmos, created by the company's Advanced Design Studios in 1954, although any of the General Motors Firebirds of that decade could possibly have provided design ideas too.

Interestingly, the idea of a flying car that can hover above the ground and fly long distances has long been a holy grail among entrepreneurs. Californian inventor Paul Moller has been working on just such a vehicle for almost 40 years, called the Skycar. Prototypes take off like a Harrier jump-jet and can then do 340mph; he has patented his baby but production has yet to start.

techniques Anderson and chums at AP Films pioneered, namely the elaborate sets, electronic lip-synching of the puppets, and the storylines rich in fantastical adventure, paved the way for later shows such as *Thunderbirds* and *Captain Scarlet & The Mysterons*. It also overcame a major problem inherent in trying to bestow puppets with realistic movement. Any kind of convincing walking was impossible to achieve; seating the tiny, handmade stars in high-tech vehicles meant they could get about without resembling old-fashioned marionettes.

And, of course, it gave us that wonderful new word to apply to exotic cars that we could only dream of owning.

Opposite: Supercar is more aircraft than automobile, as it usually hovered above the road surface.

Above: Gerry Anderson, second from left, and his *Supercar* team.

The Sweeney
Ford Consul, Granada & Cortina, Jaguar S-type

What's the link between the 1971 movie *The French Connection* and *The Sweeney*, the best contemporary TV detective series Britain has produced? Not sure? Don't worry; as the viewer, you weren't expected to notice the thread explicitly. But the tension, realism and action of William Friedkin's big-screen *The French Connection* was just what producers aimed to capture in *The Sweeney*, first shown on ITV in 1975 and whose title is the underworld's nickname for the Flying Squad.

The car chase in *The French Connection*,

in which Gene Hackman's Pontiac negotiates Brooklyn with breathtaking speed, is one of the finest in cinema history. The car chases in *The Sweeney* are some of the finest in TV history. Succinctly typified by Martin Buckley in *Classic & Sports Car* magazine as "the cat-and-mouse of the brown Consul and the S-type", they were arranged on London's mean streets by stunt gurus Peter Brayham and Frank Henson and, as Buckley comments: "An elderly Jaguar really does get semi-wasted in every episode."

But it was more than this. *The Sweeney*

producer Ted Childs wanted a true cinematic feel to the show. One of his examples: "The much-quoted shot with Gene Hackman with his paper cup standing across the street, while two drug peddlers are having a slap-up meal in a Manhattan restaurant."

The Sweeney grew out of *Regan*, a 1974 TV film written by Ian Kennedy-Martin, and starring John Thaw as tough Flying Squad Detective Inspector Jack Regan, with Dennis Waterman as his sergeant, George Carter. It was a *de facto* pilot, and the first of four series began filming the following year. There were also two *Sweeney* cinema films.

It's easy to summarise the show under the 'fags, slags, blags and Jags' slogan, but it was groundbreaking stuff. Until *The Sweeney*, even the grittiest of British cop shows had been unrealistically 'stagey'. But Euston Film's crew eschewed the studio set and took to the streets, with its fleet of cars and novel lightweight 16mm film cameras, for the ultimate in realistic action, working from tight scripts and with input from real ex-Flying Squad officers.

Self-appointed decency-arbiter Mary Whitehouse constantly criticised its violence, but Jeremy Isaacs, founder of Channel 4, rates it as "one of the most successful series ever done for British television."

Wit and wisdom of *The Sweeney*

"Get yer trousers on – you're nicked"; that classic *The Sweeney* line from John Thaw, as the no-hostages DI Regan, was first delivered not in the series but as viewers met the character in the 'Armchair Cinema' TV movie *Regan*. Thaw snarled it at a half-dressed villain shortly after breaking his door down. The scripts crackle with one-liners. As well as the immortal "Shut it!" there's also: "We're The Sweeney, son, and we haven't had any dinner." Regan and Carter's hard-drinking lifestyle is well illustrated by Carter's question: "'Ere, Guv, d'you fancy a drink?"; and Regan's riposte: "Yeah, well, the pubs are open, aren't they?"

The Flying Squad was created in 1918 – elite Scotland Yard crimebusters tasked with nabbing a newly mobile criminal fraternity. They got their name from WGT Crook, the *Daily Mail*'s chief crime reporter. An expanded Flying Squad was soon using powerful cars fitted with the first police radios. The squad evolved so that the detectives all had a driver, usually a specially-trained Traffic Division constable in plain clothes. Hence, you rarely see any Ford Consuls (in the early shows), Granadas (the later ones) or Granada MkIIs (the final episodes) driven by Carter or Regan.

Opposite: Another S-type Jag to waste.

Above: Jack Regan, the front passenger.

Left: George Carter and his back-up exit a Cortina.

Taxi
Checker cab

Taxi didn't make a star of the Checker cab. That was already a part of the fabric of New York long before this highly enjoyable US half-hour sitcom made its

A 'Checkered' career ends

The end of *Taxi* came a year after the sad demise of the Checker Motors Corporation, the Kalamazoo, Michigan-based manufacturer of the iconic New York cab which was central to the show.

The company had been building taxi cabs since 1921, and the classic model seen in *Taxi* was introduced in 1956 as the A8. It was purpose-built, although from 1960 there were passenger car versions too.

However, by the 1980s the investment needed to replace the A8 was colossal (the company had even toyed with the idea of a new cab based on a stretched Volkswagen Golf), and many cabbies had turned instead to more modern, but less characterful, Detroit-built sedans.

debut in 1978. But it did bring the diminutive actor Danny DeVito to prominence.

The series followed the ups and downs of drivers working for New York's Sunshine Cab Company – the irony being that their lives are often far from sunny, as they struggle to fulfill their dreams while transporting some of the richest people in the world. Much of working-class America knew that situation all too well. DeVito, then aged 34, plays their bad-tempered and unscrupulous boss Louie De Palma, who is the company's dispatcher following his 15 years experience as a driver.

Each show would open with the footage of a Checker cab rumbling across the Queensboro Bridge into Manhattan, and the studio set of the taxi company's garage usually featured several of the vehicles, supplied directly by the manufacturer.

Besides DeVito, the 'drivers' included Alex Reiger (played by Judd Hirsch), Elaine O'Connor-Nardo (Marilu Henner), Tony Banta (Tony Danza – a professional boxer who is also said to have driven the cab in the title sequence), and Bobby Wheeler (Jeff Conaway). But former comedian Andy Kaufmann gained many of the biggest laughs for his characterisation of Latka Gravas, the bumbling Polack whose catchphrase was "Tank-you veddy much" and who helped stoke the stereotype that all NYC cab drivers have difficulty speaking English. He also drove producers potty with his on-set strops, but his role

Taxi slipped down the rankings

Taxi was a typical example of a show adored by many critics but achieving only decent, and subsequently declining, viewer interest.

The awards rained down on it: over its run, it was nominated for 31 Emmys and won 18 of them, and received 26 Golden Globe nominations of which four became wins.

However, while the show made the number nine slot in the viewing Top 10 in the US in 1978, its first year, by 1979 it was down to 13th and a year later had fallen to 53rd position. When it was axed in 1983, it had slumped to number 73.

Danny DeVito got his starring role in *Taxi* in an unconventional way. Adopting his interpretation of the De Palma character, he marched into the audition room, slapped the script for the pilot down on the casting director's desk, and said: "Before we begin, I just wanna know one thing: who the hell wrote this piece of shit?" He got the gig instantly.

proved so popular that they usually accommodated his demands.

Alex Reiger, meanwhile, is the anchor, dolefully resigned to his place in life – indeed, in his chaotic life, his job is the one constant – while his colleagues bitch and moan about their lot, usually after work at Mario's bar. In fact, storylines did cover such real-life issues as drug abuse, teenage runaways and bereavement.

Taxi was to remain in the schedules until 1983. There were 114 episodes, the first four seasons shown on ABC before an ill-starred switch to NBC that saw viewing figures nosedive towards the cancellation of one more series. Two writers and a director who worked together on the show left to create bar-room sitcom *Cheers*.

Opposite: Danny DeVito, on left, with the cast of US sit-com *Taxi*, clustered around one of Sunshine Cab Company's workhorses.

Thunderbirds

Rolls-Royce 'FAB 1'

Every tiny detail of Gerry Anderson's miniature future-world has been analysed by aficionados, including the superbly detailed sets, spectacular and ground-breaking special effects, and the vivid puppet characterisations of the Tracy clan and its International Rescue organisation. It's probably the most discussed and best-loved kids' show of all time.

But, oddly for a series where much of the action takes place in the skies or in space, the mechanical star of the show remains a car... and probably the most famous 'star' of the show is its owner.

We're talking Lady Penelope or, more precisely, Lady Penelope Creighton-Ward, the British-based affiliate of Jeff Tracy and his courageous sons Scott, Virgil, Alan, Gordon and John. She was originally intended to be voiced by Fenella Fielding until Anderson's wife and co-producer, Sylvia, instead brought her to

A 'FAB 1' for real life

Besides the two small versions of 'FAB 1' used in the making of *Thunderbirds*, there was a third, larger one.

In 1966, and to promote the cinematic opening of the feature film *Thunderbird 6* around the UK, Gerry Anderson commissioned a real-life six-wheeled Rolls-Royce. It was bodied in metal and fully roadgoing, its twin front-wheel steering system coming from the same type of Bedford coach that featured at the cliffhanger end of the classic 1969 movie *The Italian Job*. Today, Anderson now thinks the car is "hideous".

It toured the country along with Penny Snow, a Lady Penelope lookalike, in 1967 and '68. Many years later, the car was painstakingly restored and now takes pride of place in the Cars Of The Stars Museum in Keswick, Cumbria.

Both movie versions of the TV original, *Thunderbirds Are Go* and *Thunderbird 6* were well received, but proved unexpected box office flops. However, the latter featured one of the most intricate shots ever produced for Gerry Anderson's 'Supermarionation' shows, when the flying craft Thunderbirds 1, 2 and 6 travel in convoy with the Rolls-Royce. A set had to be specially constructed and ran the length of the Slough studio floor.

glamorous life. Her shifty Cockney chauffeur Parker stole his fair share of scenes too.

When Gerry Anderson conceived the show for ATV as a follow-up to his previous puppet shows, he decided Lady P would need transport to reflect her adventurous lifestyle. The task of designing it fell to special effects supervisor Derek Meddings, who was told to produce a "Rolls-Royce for the 21st century." This was after Gerry Anderson had visited a

Opposite: 'FAB 1' – all seven feet of the original, bright pink studio model.

Above, left: A helping hand shows the scale of Lady Penelope and Parker puppets.

factory which armour-plated cars to get an idea of what would be involved.

Meddings certainly gave it a huge range of abilities, as the car could dispense walls of smoke, and fire rockets from a cannon behind its radiator grille. But four features stand out: first, it is bright pink; second, it has six wheels; third; it has a transparent canopy on top; and fourth, it *is* actually a Rolls-Royce.

The Crewe-based manufacturer gave its permission for Anderson to use its name on his car. It even provided a real-life grille for close-up shots of rocket-firing. Obviously, Rolls-Royce knew the show would promote its cars globally, because TV legend Lew Grade was right behind the project – indeed, he loved the first half-hour show so much that he ordered Anderson to extend it to an hour on twice the budget. He's said to have bellowed: "That's not a television series, it's a feature film!" RR also

liked the advanced equipment it boasted. But there was one proviso: it must always, always be referred to as a "Rolls-Royce" and never, perish the thought, as a "Roller" or "Rolls".

For the 32 episodes, two versions of the car were made, a tiny one about 6in long for inclusion in model sets, and another – the definitive one – a 7ft-long model for filming in scenes featuring the puppets themselves. This version was built, at a cost of £3,000, by Arthur Evans of special effects suppliers Mastermodels, and was constructed from wood and plywood. Bicycle lights were used for the headlights, and the tyres were specially cast in rubber

The actual shape of the car is interesting: Gerry Anderson was an enthusiastic owner of a Jaguar Mk10, while Barry Gray, who composed the superb theme music for *Thunderbirds,* owned a Facel Vega. Traces of both cars can be seen in it.

The car was given the number plate 'FAB 1'. This matched the "F.A.B." radio sign-off, in place of "Roger", that all the characters used when communicating, but has no meaning. Gerry Anderson was always rather bemused by questions about "F.A.B.", explaining it was nothing more than the popular shortening of 'fabulous' that was fashionable in the mid-1960s, and was just meant to sound hip.

Rolls-Royce denied producers of the recent *Thunderbirds* live-action movie the right to use its name. Instead, Ford produced a pink six-wheeled 'FAB 1' car for the film... to the scorn of fans and Gerry Anderson alike!

HUDSON: the unknown puppet Rolls

Gerry Anderson once again teamed up with Rolls-Royce in 1983 during the making of his puppet show *Terrahawks.*

The car was known as 'HUDSON'; nothing to do with the American marque last seen in the early 1950s, but standing for 'Heuristic Universal Driver with Sensory and Orbital Navigation). Chameleon-like, its body could change colour – achieved by covering it in tiny glass beads to reflect coloured studio lights.

It was built by contractor Space Models at a cost of £7,500, although a studio set of its interior for the puppets to sit in cost double that.

Below: This real-life 'FAB 1' carried Lady Penelope lookalike Penny Snow around the UK to promote a *Thunderbirds* movie.